WHERE DUTY CALLS
The Story of
Sarah Emma Edmonds
Soldier and Spy
in the Union Army

by
MARILYN SEGUIN

BRANDEN PUBLISHING COMPANY
Boston

Library of Congress Cataloging-in-Publication Data

Seguin, Marilyn.
   Where duty calls : the story of Sarah Emma Edmonds,
soldier and spy in the Union Army / by Marilyn Seguin.
      p. cm.
   Includes bibliographical references and index.
   ISBN 0-8283-2047-0 (alk. paper)
   1. Edmonds, S. Emma E. (Sarah Emma Evelyn), 1841-
1898 Fiction.
   2. United States--History--Civil War, 1861-1865--Partici-
pation, Female Fiction.
   3. United States--History--Civil War, 1861-1865--Secret
service Fiction.
   I. Title.
   PS3569.E454W48 1999
   813'.54--dc21   99-25956
                                                    CIP

Branden Publishing Company
17 Station Street
PO Box 843 Brookline Village
Boston, MA 02447

Sarah Emma Edmonds (left) and Sarah as Franklin Thompson (right). (Photos courtesy of State Archives of Michigan).

Contents

Dedication:

In memory of the hundreds of women who fought in disguise beside their male compatriots during the American Civil War.

"They went where duty seemed to call,
 They scarcely asked the reason why;
 They only knew they could but die,
And death was not the worst of all!"

John Greenleaf Whittier

"There was a strong bond of sympathy between us (Emma and James V.), for we both believed that duty called us there, and were willing to lay down even life itself, if need be, in this glorious cause."

The Female Spy, p. 99

Now is the judgment of this world. Each man and woman is taking his or her measure. As it is taken even so must it stand--it will be recorded. The activities of war quicken into life every evil propensity as well as every good principle.
--Hannah Ropes, *Civil War Nurse*, December 14, 1862.

Preface

In the aftermath of Gettysburg, thousands of bodies littered the bloodstained fields. In one section of the battlefield, where the infamous Pickett's Charge took place, a burial detail worked, handkerchiefs tied over their mouths to block the hideous stench of rotting human flesh in the hot July sun. Among the bodies, the burial detail found that of a woman clad in the butternut gray of the Confederacy. The burial detail might have thought the face was that of a young boy had not the clothing been so blown away to reveal the young woman's breasts.

More than seventy years later, a Civil War grave site was discovered on the outskirts of the Shiloh National Military Park, which contained the remains of nine Union soldiers. One of the bodies was that of a female, and a minie ball was found with her remains, leaving little doubt that she died in battle.

Historians estimate that at least 400 women enlisted and fought on both sides during the terrible national conflict that was the War Between the States. Their reasons for enlisting ranged from wanting to stay with husbands or lovers to patriotism and a firm dedication to the cause for which they fought. Most of these women disguised themselves as men, and some were soon discovered and discharged. Clara Barton reported treating a young woman soldier for her injuries after the battle of Antietam, only discovering her gender when removing the woman's clothing to treat her wound. Several other women soldiers went undiscovered until they delivered babies.

A few women fought in the war and their identity was never discovered. **Where Duty Calls** is a fictionalized account of one of those young women, Sarah Emma Edmonds (born Edmonson, a.k.a. Frank Thompson), whose identity was apparently never revealed until many years after the war ended. Emma's experience is especially interesting because during her enlistment she served as a Union spy, causing her to adopt multiple identities in addition to her male disguise. What we know of her life and exploits during this time is recorded in her memoirs, **The Female Spy of the Union Army**, and in the excellent biography **She Rode With Generals**, by Sylvia Dannett.

Where Duty Calls is a work of fiction based upon Emma's memoirs, and as such, depends upon the author's imagination for some of the dialogue and details. Quotes from Emma's memoirs, however, are authentic and credited by page reference to **The Female Spy**.

Marilyn Seguin, Cuyahoga Falls, Ohio, January 1999

Sarah Emma Evelyn Edmonds

Emma's birth . . . . December 1841

Civil War begins . . . . April 1861

Emma's enlistment in Company F . . . . May 1861
Second Michigan Regiment
Volunteer Infantry

Lieutenant James Vesey's death . . . . April 1862

Execution of Union spy Timothy . . . . April 1862
Webster in Richmond

Emma volunteers as spy . . . . May 1862

Emma leaves the army . . . . April 1863
and resumes female identity

End of Civil War . . . . April 1865

Emma marries Linus H. Seelye . . . . April 1867

Emma receives an honorable discharge . . . . . . July 1884
resulting in a Special Act of
Congress that grants her a Veteran's
pension

Emma's death . . . . September 1898

Battles in Which Emma Served as Frank Thompson

First Bull Run (First Manassas), Va., July 1861

Williamsburg, Va., May 1862

Battle of Fair Oaks (Seven Pines), Va., May 1862

Seven Days' Battles around Richmond, Va., June and July 1862

Second Bull Run, Va., August 1862

Antietam, Md., Sept. 1862

Fredericksburg, Va., Dec. 1862

Vicksburg, Miss., March 1863

Chapter 1
ESCAPE FROM BONDAGE

Emma hoisted the heavy bag over her shoulder in the pre dawn gloom, picked up her heaviest pair of shoes, and quietly crept to the bedroom door. The bag was heavy, but precious, and she had chosen its contents carefully, hiding it under the bed until moments ago when she felt it was safe to finally escape. Inside was everything she would need to start her new life--money for the stage coach ticket, a sandwich and an apple, a few dresses, underwear, her journal, and her tattered copy of *Fanny Campbell, The Female Pirate Captain, A Tale of the Revolution!*

Slowly and silently so as not to awaken her older sister Rebecca with whom she shared the room, she opened the door and tip-toed down the long narrow hallway of the old farmhouse, past her parents' closed bedroom door, past her brother Thomas' room, being careful not to step on any of the floorboards that might creak. Slowly, she made her way down the staircase, counting each of the fourteen steps that led down to the heavy door at the front entryway.

At the bottom of the steps, Emma stopped and looked to the right into the parlor with its cold fireplace and furniture that Mother kept covered except when they had guests. Emma gasped at the reflected image in the mirror over the fireplace. At first she thought that the narrow face with the deep set eyes staring back at her was Mother, her dear face faded old before her time. But then she realized it was her own face looking back at her from the smoky glass.

Emma inspected her image that was reflected in the early morning half light. She saw a tall girl with a flat bosom, thin arms and legs, and a straight nose. Her hair was tied back with a piece of plain ribbon. Emma knew that her smile was her only display of femininity. At best, she could be described as handsome, but for a girl that description was the same as plain. Emma breathed a silent good bye to her home, and opened the door.

Outside, Emma made her way to the clothesline, where yesterday's laundry still hung, damp with dew from the cool New Brunswick night air. Shivering, she shed her nightgown and took from the clothesline a pair of her brother Thomas' work pants and one of his heavy, plaid shirts. She dressed in Thomas' clothes, pulled on her shoes, and stuffed her long brown hair into the crown of a wide-brimmed straw hat that would keep the sun off her face later in the day. In this outfit she had to pass for a boy, for no Canadian girl traveled alone in 1856.

Satisfied with her appearance, Emma clipped to the clothesline the farewell note she had written the night before. Mother would be sure to find it when she gathered in the clothes.

Dear Mother,

By the time you find this note, I will be safely away from Magaguadavic and Pa's wretched plan to marry me to the awful Farmer Bolton. I have no desire to share my life with any man, especially not old Farmer Bolton, who must be 30 at least, twice my age. You must not worry, for I have a plan, and I will write once I am settled. Please give my love to my brother and sisters (but not to Pa) and tell James that I will write him also. Forgive me, but this is for the best.

Your loving daughter,
Emma

Emma was sorry to have to hurt her mother by her leaving, but there was just no reasoning with Pa. Emma's mother, Betsy Leeper, with her red hair and gentle ways, had come to Canada from Ireland and married the head-strong Scotsman Isaac Edmonson when she was just sixteen. Their first child, Eliza, was born soon after. To Isaac's great disappointment three more girls, Frances, Mary Jane and Rebecca, were born in quick succession. Then a fifth daughter was born and Betsy named her Sarah Emma, but called her Emma after Betsy's own mother.

Isaac was so frustrated at the lack of a son that he became a tyrant in his own household, often resorting to violence to keep his wife and daughters "in line." The birth of Thomas a year after Sarah Emma did little to soften Isaac's disposi-tion towards the females of his household. As Thomas grew, the boy too turned out to be a disappointment in Isaac's eyes. Thomas was of little use around the farm because he was frail and suffered from frequent seizures that were terrifying to his mother.

As long as Emma stayed in Magaguadavic, she knew her father would continue to goad her into marriage--if not with the despicable Farmer Bolton, then with someone else. I'd rather be dead, thought Emma, than live like Mother, always at the beck and call of Pa, always having to please Pa and never having any pleasure for herself. A slave to Pa, that was what Mother was, thought Emma.

Emma wasn't impressed by her oldest sisters' marriages either. Eliza had married John Miller when Emma was a little girl, and Eliza looked and acted weary and old all the time. Mary Jane had married Henry Davidson and moved away, and Frances was married to James Saunders who owned the neighboring farm. At nineteen, Frances already had three children and she'd almost died giving birth to the last one. No thanks, thought Emma. I'll not be risking my life to have children when I'm but fifteen.

"Let Farmer Bolton marry Rebecca," Emma had suggested to her father. "She's older than I am. She should get married next."

"You'll marry him, yerself. It's you he's asked for, lassie," said Isaac, and Emma dared not talk back to him for she feared his hot anger. One time Rebecca had sassed Pa when he'd asked her why her chores weren't done, and Pa'd nearly knocked Rebecca off her feet with a quick cuff at her head. Only one of his household Pa'd never roughed up was Thomas, even when Thomas made Pa angry. Emma puzzled over how Pa could keep his temper in control with Thomas but not with the rest of his family, not even Ma.

"I won't marry him," Emma later declared to her mother.

"Then ye must marry someone else, for we can't keep ye forever, Emma Edmonson, and marryin' is the only way for a woman to leave her parents," said her mother.

"But he's so old, Mother. He already has two children by his wife that died. I'm not ready to be marrying anybody."

Mother had looked at Emma sadly, and said, "Och, Emma, ye must try to make the best out of things ye cannot avoid. That is the duty of a woman."

"Not this woman," Emma muttered.

And so Emma had thought about her situation and decided to run away. It seemed the only way to avoid Pa and the dreadful Farmer Bolton, that's for sure, but she would be sorry to hurt her gentle mother. Emma, at age fifteen, already had a reputation for being headstrong and willful, and she was sorry that she had always been such a worry to her mother who had enough other things to worry about. Once, after church Emma had heard her mother talking to Reverend McDonald about her.

"Of all my children, I fear most for my youngest daughter, Emma, who is always up to some mischief or other," Mother said.

"And wout kind a mischief will 'at be?" asked the elderly Rev. McDonald.

"Emma chooses risk and danger in all she does," said Ma. "She rides the wildest horse on the farm, climbs the tallest trees. I fear she will meet some violent end."

Rev. McDonald had comforted Ma. "It is an auld saying, an' I believe a true one, 'A wean that's born to be hung 'ill ne'er be droon'd.'" And then the old Reverend had turned to Emma, and laying his hand on her head, said in his best Scottish dialect: "But, me wee lassie, ya don't tempt Providence wi' your madcap antics, or ye may no live oot half your days."

Unlike her sisters, Emma had never been content with the domestic chores or the routine farm life to which she was born. Leave the washing, canning, and sewing to Eliza, Frances, Mary Jane and Rebecca. Emma preferred the outside life--roaming the woods with her brother Thomas and their friend James Vesey, fishing in the nearby river, galloping the horses through the fields on a rabbit hunt. Her sisters laughed at her for her "unfeminine ways," but Thomas and James encouraged her in her physical feats--like running across the Vesey's field where the bull lived or riding the most vicious horse on the farm.

The farmhouse suffocated Emma, and she slept outside in the barn when Betsy would allow it. When Betsy didn't allow it, Emma sometimes snuck out there anyway, getting up early to comb the hay out of her hair and sneak back into the house before anyone was the wiser.

Not bothering to tuck in the shirt, Emma hoisted her bag over her shoulder once again and made her way towards the barn to say good bye to Maggie. The old border collie wagged her tail in greeting as Emma spoke to her.

"Take care of yourself, old girl. And don't chase the hens or Pa'll beat you," warned Emma, as she scratched the dog behind her ears. Last week, Pa had come home to find Maggie inside the chicken pen, herding up the frightened, squawking hens as if they were sheep. Pa had raised his rifle and aimed at Maggie, squeezed off a shot, but missed. At the sound of the shot, the dog had stopped her herding, and was sitting in the midst of the frantic hens as Pa raised his rifle a second time. Emma and her sisters had pleaded with Isaac not to shoot their pet.

"Scared hens don't lay eggs," said Isaac, as he took aim.

In the end only the desperate pleas of Thomas saved Maggie from a bloody death by her own master. Now Emma hugged her pet. "Be good, Maggie," she said. The dog looked at Emma adoringly and rose to follow her out of the barn.

"Stay, girl," said Emma, and Maggie obediently lay down in the hay and rested her head on her paws.

Then Emma followed the long tree-lined driveway to the gravel road that strung together the farms of rural Magaguadavic. If she was lucky, she would be able to hitch a ride to town on a farmer's wagon. In the east she saw the sky begin to turn rosy. She'd have to hurry. A gust of wind ballooned her shirt and Emma felt exhilarated with the freedom from the tight-bodiced dresses she was accustomed to wearing.

At noon, Emma rested in the shade of a stand of pines, and munched her sandwich. The day was golden, warm and bright, and it matched her mood as she thought about her future. At home by now, they would know she had left for good. Her mother would have found the note pinned to the clothesline, and she would tell Isaac when he came in from chores for his noonday meal. Isaac would be angry. She hoped her mother would be careful and keep her distance.

Suddenly, the sound of a wagon on the road made Emma tense, and she froze where she sat, waiting to see who was coming. When she saw that it was only a young boy and his dog driving a hay wagon, she stood up and went to the road to wave him down.

"Can I ride with you a piece?" she asked as the boy slowed the horses to a stop. The dog jumped off the seat and sniffed around Emma but did not bark.

"Makin' a hay delivery to town," said the boy. "You're welcome to ride in the wagon."

Emma thanked him and climbed up into the hay, amused that the dog followed her instead of returning to the wagon seat with its master. At least she'd have good company on the long, bumpy ride to Magaguadavic Siding, where she could catch a stage coach to Saint John. From there, she would take a river boat to Salisbury.

Emma had saved whatever coins she could get by bargaining produce and eggs with the local merchants, but she had been careful not to make Pa suspicious. If Pa found out she was keeping some of the money for herself, he would beat her for stealing. Last night she had counted her money, and she had exactly the right amount to purchase her coach and river boat fares. Emma took it as a sign from God that she should pack up and go as soon as possible.

Soon, a train would come through Magaguadavic Siding, her friend James had told her, and travel would be easy. Emma had questioned him closely about the train, how fast it went, where it would make stops. James, who often took the train when visiting relatives in the United States, had explained to her.

"First, you need a schedule, so's you know when the train departs and arrives at certain places," he said. In time, James had obliged her by procuring one of the mysterious schedules, and using his pocket watch, had showed her how to interpret the rows and columns of numbers according to clock time.

"You can buy tickets two ways, round trip or one way. We always buy round trip cause that way we only buy once and we get back home again," said James, closing the lid of his watch and replacing it in the pocket of his grimy overalls. "Why you so interested in trains, anyway, Emma? You goin' somewhere?" James had asked.

Emma had been evasive. "Someday, I want to see the world," she said. "Not just Canada and the United States, either. They have trains in Europe you know, and I'll need to know how to buy a ticket if I'm to ride the train." Emma believed in destiny and she believed in God and His will. God, she knew, often gave signs that a course of action was right or wrong. She would wait for the right sign before she left Magaguavadic.

But Emma didn't tell James that Farmer Bolton had paid her a call, or that she had overheard her Pa and the old farmer discussing marriage plans that involved her. She didn't want James' advice on this particular problem, no siree. This is one problem she would take care of herself. But figuring out a train schedule was a different thing, and she needed his help. Emma now wished she had said goodbye to James. She would miss her dearest friend and companion.

In town, Emma paid her fare and boarded the stagecoach. No one recognized her in Thomas' clothes, and she felt smug about her trickery for she had passed several of her neighbors on the street. She took out her apple, munched it, dropped the core out the window and watched as it hit the dirt and rolled under the coach. Emma reached inside her bag and pulled out her journal, and she began to write:

June 5, 1856

Today I have escaped bondage and am finally free.

Chapter 2
A Letter from James

September 5, 1856
Dearest Mother,

You will be happy to know that I am finally settled here with cousin Annie Moffit, and I am going to school to learn the millinery trade. You probably will get a good laugh over my choice of profession, as I never took much interest in such frippery when I lived on the farm. I am grateful that the rest of the world, if not myself, feels only partially dressed if they are not wearing a bonnet. My teachers say my work is very good. At any rate, the millinery trade will allow me to earn my own living as I have little interest in ever being supported by another.

As soon as I have finished learning the trade, Annie and I plan to find jobs in Moncton, and we may even become partners in a business already established there owned by Annie's friend, Henriette Perrigo. Do you know her? She is a most pleasant woman, though overly stout and frequently out of breath. Henriette absolutely gushes over my work and says she would be most happy to have me and Annie come the first of the year.

Please convey my love to my sisters and Thomas, and tell them to write, but do not give them my address. You can forward their letters with your own, as that will lessen the chances of Pa's finding me.

Your loving daughter,
Emma

P.S. Next time James comes to see Thomas, tell him I am well.
P.S.S. Please address future letters to Emma Edmonds. I thought it best to change my name in case Pa comes looking for me.

Moncton was a thriving, active town, and Emma and Annie enjoyed the sights and sounds of the city when they were not actually working, which was most of the time.

Moncton gave Emma her first experience of life in the big city, and she explored it with the same relish and vigor with which she had explored the woods and fields of Magaguadavic. Henriette soon gave up her insistence at accompanying the girls on their explorations after one excursion so sapped her strength that she had to stay in bed for a week.

In her cousin Annie, Emma found a true friend. Like Emma, Annie enjoyed traipsing around the city, taking in the sights. When the weather prevented them from roaming the city streets in their off hours, they stayed in their cozy apartment over the millinery shop and read. Emma and Annie took turns reading from their only book, Emma's copy of the novel *Fanny Campbell, The Female Pirate Captain, A Tale of the Revolution!* They thrilled to the adventures of the heroine Fanny who, disguised as Seaman Channing, sets out to rescue her imprisoned lover.

"Poor lovesick girl," said Emma, after Annie had finished reading the chapter in which Fanny cut off her curls and assumed a male persona.

"The story is rather far-fetched, don't you agree?" said Annie. "Surely, no girl has done all the things that author Ballou has Fanny do."

But Emma disagreed. In her heart she knew that, like Fanny, if given the chance Emma Edmonds could row a boat, shoot a panther, or ride the wildest horses in the province.

Emma also read the newspapers every day, hoping always to catch some news of anyone in Magaguadavic, for her mother's letters were few, and she could not write home often herself in case her father should intercept the mail. Her mother wrote her when she could, and once had forwarded a note from James.

Dear Em,

You scowndrell!! If me and Thomas had a clue about your runaway plans, we'd have gone with you. Tom says your Pa is real mad cause he wanted to marry you off to Farmer Bolton. If you decide to come home, I will marry you so you don't have to hook up with that old man. If you decide to take me up on the offer, you'll still have to look out for your father. He is real mad that you stole the egg money. Hope you are well. Me and Thomas miss you a lot.

Your best friend,
James V.

P.S. Maggie doesn't run in the woods with me and Tom anymore. I think she misses you too.

Emma read the letter twice. She closed her eyes and thought about the life she had left behind. As much as she loved the city, she still missed the woods and fields of Magaguadavic. She also missed her friend James. She remembered one of the last times she had seen him.

On that afternoon, after a wild race on horseback through the woods, the two youngsters had rested in a grassy field near the Edmondson farm. Emma gloated because once again she had won the race.

"You're just lucky, is all," said James. "My horse is always faster than yours on the roads."

"I don't believe luck has a thing to do with it, James," Emma replied, smugly. "What'll happen, will happen anyway. I believe in destiny, and my destiny is to live a life of adventure."

"A little luck wouldn't hurt, though, now would it?" said James, chewing on a piece of grass.

Emma smiled at him, and rolled over on her stomach in the grass. She ran her hand over a spot of ground. Then she plucked something from the grass and presented it to her friend.

"Well then, Master James, may this forever bring you the luck you think you need," she said as she presented him a perfect four leaf clover.

James pulled out his pocket watch and opened a hinged cover on the back. He placed the clover inside the cover and closed it with a snap. "I'll save it for a time when it's needed, to be sure, Emma Edmondson," he said.

Emma reread James' letter and thought about that day, that perfect golden afternoon. James, cautious, wise and gentle, always thought things through carefully before taking action. He was not impetuous and headstrong as Emma was. How had he been able to stand her? Oh, how she wished she could see her old friend, but to visit him would be far too risky and she dared not write him in case her letter be intercepted and her whereabouts discovered. Although Emma never answered James' letter, she shared it with her cousin.

"Will you marry James then?" asked Annie.

"Marry? That's what I was running away from, remember?" answered Emma.

But Emma secretly wondered what it would be like married to James. There had been times they had stolen a few kisses and hugs at parties and dances, and once she had been jealous to hear that James was courting another.

"I heard you been spooning with Sallie MacGregor," she had said to him.

"What's it to you if I am?" he'd asked her, but not in a mean way.

"Nothing. Just heard it, is all," she'd replied. It wouldn't do to have James think she cared about it. He was just a friend. "She sure is a pretty girl," said Emma after a while.

"Who is?"

"Sallie MacGregor."

"Yep, I suppose," said James. And they never spoke of Sallie MacGregor again.

Mostly, Emma thought of James as a companion in adventure. He was someone to go riding through the woods with, or to hunt and fish with. Still, being married to James might not be so bad if they could always have adventures like those.

"Perhaps one day I'll ask James to marry me," Emma said to her cousin. "After I have seen the world."

The millinery shop was a busy place, for most men and women in the year 1858 wore head coverings at all times of the year. Women's hats changed with the season, and every new gown purchase required a visit to the millinery shop for a matching bonnet order. The fashion now was the jocket hat, a round-crowned head covering with a small, curved brim decorated with a feather, usually from the tail of a rooster, but Emma and Annie used ostrich feathers when they could get them.

Most of the men wore stove pipe hats, also called top hats, which sat high upon their heads, exposing their ears in the cold Canadian winters. Emma was content with her work for the time being, and she saved what she could for her future.

And then one day, Emma received a message from her mother that turned her well ordered, contented life topsy turvy.

May 5, 1858
My Dearest Emma,
I am writing in haste to warn you of that which you need to know to safeguard your future. Last week, your father went to Harvey town to buy grain, and met up with some acquaintances of Annie's. Somehow the talk got around to you, and your father put two and two together. As he now suspects you are with Annie, it can't be long until he discovers your true where-abouts. Your father is steadfast in his intent to marry you to Mr. Bolton to spite you for running away. Take care daughter.
Your loving mother,
Betsy E.

Emma shared this letter with Annie.

"You must return to Magaguadavic at once and marry James," she advised.

"Never. I shall not rush to the arms of one man to avoid another. I have no need of any man as yet," said Emma.

"Then you must go to Salisbury. I will contact friends who will let you stay with them until your father settles down. Then you can come back to Moncton," said Annie.

"If Pa can track me to Moncton, he can track me to Salisbury as well," said Emma. "I can't stay here, but I will make the best out of what I can't avoid. I will go to the

United States--it will be a beginning of the traveling adventure that I had planned all along," said Emma.

"But how will you live? You know no one in the United States, and surely you've not yet saved enough money to open a millinery shop of your own," protested Annie.

"I have a plan," said Emma, as she took down her copy of *Fanny Campbell* from the book shelf and pulled out a newspaper clipping that she had tucked between the pages. She handed the clipping to Annie.

Book Agents Wanted
United States Publisher needs agents to canvass for
New Pictorial, Standard and Historical and Religious
works. Good men will confer a public BENEFIT and
receive a FAIR COMPENSATION for their labour. To
persons of enterprise and tact this business offers an
opportunity for profitable employment seldom to be
met with. Persons wishing to engage in their sale will
be received for interviews immediately.
L.P. Crown and Company, Publishers
Boston, Massachusetts

"Imagine being able to roam the continent and get paid for it!" Emma said. "It's the perfect solution. I believe this was meant to be, Annie. This ad is a sign that I should begin my traveling adventures!"

"Oh, Emma, you can't be serious," said Annie, clearly shocked at her cousin's words. "This ad says men are wanted, not women. No female would be safe journeying across the continent peddling books."

Emma said nothing, but held up the book she and Annie had so often read in the evenings by candlelight. Annie looked at the book and then at Emma's face, and shook her head in disbelief.

"You'll interview for the job as a man?" Annie whispered, incredulous. "Oh no Emma, you can't. Fanny Campbell is just a character in a book. She's a fiction, Emma. What works in fiction won't work in real life!" exclaimed Annie.

In the end, it was Annie who cut off Emma's long hair. And on the day Emma left for the United States, Annie helped Emma wind the wide cotton band that flattened her breasts under the dapper new suit coat that Emma had purchased for her interview. Emma Edmonds, a.k.a. Frank Thompson, age 19, boarded the train for Boston.

Chapter 3
Emma Goes to War

Flint, Michigan
December 1860

Dear Mother,

You shall be comforted to know that my work as book seller has placed me in the field of "foreign missionary," work for which I feel I was destined. I have prospered by selling Bibles here in the West, but in the East everyone seems to already own at least one Bible.

You must not worry that I am lonely in my disguise, for I assure you that I have found kind friends of both sexes here, though I pretty much keep to myself in my free time.

I love my work and this country, though recent talk of war may threaten the best interests of my adopted nation. South Carolina has voted to secede from the Union, and other states may follow their example. It is all everyone talks about.

A happy Christmas to you and my brother and sisters. Please tell James when you see him that I am well, but do not tell him of my disguise or whereabouts.

Love,
Emma

P.S. Continue to address future letters to Frank Thompson until further notice.

Lincoln declares insurrection, not war

Washington D.C., April 15,1861

Carefully avoiding use of the word "war," President Lincoln today declared a state of "insurrection" as he issued an appeal for 75,000 volunteers for three months of military service. His call for troops came only a day after the fall of Fort Sumter into the hands of the Confederate militia.

In his proclamation today, the President called for "all loyal citizens" to defend "the Union and to redress wrongs already long enough endured."

Ten days later, Emma watched the departure of the first troops to answer the President's call. The regiments were drawn up in a line, their bright bayonets flashing in the morning sunlight. Emma stood on the corner of Kearsley and Saginaw Streets with the crowd, and bowed her head as the Pastor delivered a farewell message to the troops. Then he presented a New Testament to each soldier, inscribed with the words of Oliver Cromwell: "My men, put your trust in the Lord, and keep your powder dry."

A representative of The Committee of Ladies pinned a badge of red, white and blue rosettes, bearing the inscription "The Union and the Constitution," on the breast of each soldier. The volunteers of Company F, First Michigan, United States Army, were now ready to go off to war.

Emma thought her heart would break as she witnessed the final goodbyes and embraces of those who had come to say farewell to their loved ones, perhaps forever. Many of the women were openly weeping, and children and babies were clinging to their fathers and grandfathers. Then came the order to march, and amid the cheers of the spectators and the strains of the "Star Spangled Banner," the new recruits moved forward on their way to Washington D.C.

So they were going to fight battles, thought Emma, and she thrilled at the vision of glory that filled her head. She had read of battle heroics and marches and bravery in the field and she longed to be a part of it. The coming strife was a large thing, a great movement full of honor and valor. Emma cheered on the marching soldiers, exhilarated by the music and the waving banners and the blue and brass of the uniforms. When the last line of soldiers withdrew from sight and the band stopped playing, only the sobbing was to be heard. Emma, in her disguise as Frank Thompson, could only thank God that she was free to answer the call to duty and was not obliged to stay home and weep.

The next morning at eight o'clock, Emma, a.k.a. Frank Thompson, walked to the Armory to enlist. She looked at the men in line, some hardly more than boys. She watched as one youngster, who couldn't have been a day over sixteen, wrote the number 18 on a slip of paper and put it in his shoe. When the enlistment officer asked the boy if he was over eighteen, the boy had replied confidently, "Yes, sir, I **swear** that I'm over eighteen."

"Then you're old enough to fight the Rebels, boy," the officer declared.

Emma was confident that her naturally husky voice and her recent haircut gave her the look of a teenage boy, rather than the 19-year-old woman that she was. When it came time for the physical exam, a nervous Emma stood in line with the other young men enlistees, awaiting her turn.

"Stand up straight," said the doctor. Then he gave her two taps on the chest, turned her around, and ran his hands over her shoulders, back, and limbs. Finally, he whirled her back around to face him and said, "Frank Thompson, you are all right and fit for the service. I only wish we had a hundred such fine boys as you!"

Emma took the oath of allegiance with her fellow volunteers:

> *I do solemnly swear in the presence of Almighty God that I will support the Constitution of the United States and maintain it and my country's flag, if necessary, with my life; that I will obey the commands of my superior officers while in service; and will defend and protect my comrades in battle to the best of my physical ability; --so help me God.*

Emma Edmonds was now ready to go to war. There was no doubt in her mind that it was her destiny.

Chapter 4
New Friends

New Brunswick, Canada
May 31, 1861
My dear child,

I take time to write to you to let you know that your family is well. I received a letter from you today and I was much displeased. I implore you to give up this ruse and come home at once. This war is not yours, my child. Leave it to the Americans who fight each other, most foolishly, in my opinion.

If you will not leave the war, at least then leave that which causes you the most danger, and which must surely be your most constant trouble--that of seeming to be what you are not. Cast off the Yankee uniform and take back your skirts, Emma. Or if you must stay in this war, at least stay as the woman you are.

I pray daily for your safety. And I pray for the swift resolution to this foolish war which is surely ripping your adopted country apart.

Your loving mother,
Betsy Edmonds

P.S. Thomas has just told me that James Vesey has left Magaguadavic for the U.S.A. to join up in the fighting. I can only thank God that Thomas' seizures must bar him from any such pursuits.

P.S.S. Please do not write to me again until you can sign your own rightful name to your letter.

Sarah Emma Edmonds, a.k.a. Private Frank Thompson, sighed and replaced her mother's letter in its envelope. Betsy Edmonds would never understand what drove her daughter.

On the way to Washington, Emma's enthusiasm grew. Citizens cheered them as they marched through the streets. In each town they passed through, the people provided great stores of cold meat, cheeses, bread and coffee. Emma began to believe that she was on a great mission in service to her adopted country, and if her enthusiasm was any measure of the zeal of the army, surely this war could not last long.

They marched cheerfully on to Washington and set up camp. The weather was perfect. The beautiful wooded heights were crowned with white tents and the dust hung lazily over the drill grounds and roadways. Every afternoon the military bands performed, filling the sun washed air with stirring martial music. The camps were thronged with visitors, some who had traveled long distances to be with their friends and relatives in the army.

The troops settled into their tents and the immense force that would soon be known as the Army of the Potomac began to concentrate on instruction. They included shoemakers, clerks, mechanics, teamsters and teachers, now turned soldiers, every one. During the day, the soldiers drilled. At night they played cards, read, and wrote letters home, waiting, waiting for the day they would receive marching orders so they could be about the business they came for--fighting.

While in camp, Emma kept to herself as much as possible. At night, she was forced to share one of the circular Sibley tents with eleven other enlisteds. The bell-shaped structure was supported by a center pole, and its inhabitants arranged themselves for sleep in the manner of wheel spokes, feet at the center, and heads near the canvas walls. Emma slept in the same clothes she wore during the day.

Sometimes, the men stripped naked and bathed in the stream called Bull Run. Emma, however, waited until taps sounded, and then crept quietly from the tent and made her way to the stream to bathe alone. She used a private toilet area, avoiding the common "sinks" or long open trenches used by most of the troops. There was no doubt that should her sex be discovered, Emma would be expelled from service, so Emma was careful to remain in character.

Emma, as "Frank Thompson," was assigned duty as a nurse in the regimental hospital, a position she had asked for. The majority of the nurses were men, and during the days before the battles began, they spent most of their time digging drains around the hospital tent. But during the blistering heat of June, typhoid began to take its toll on the soldiers in camp, and Emma found fulfillment in her service to the sick.

From Emma's *Memoirs*:

> *June 10, 1861*
> *...my labors began in earnest, and as I went from tent to tent ministering to the wants of those delirious, helpless men, I wondered if there ever was a "Missionary Field" which promised a richer harvest than the one in which I am already engaged; and oh, how thankful I am that it was my privilege to take some small part in so great a work.*
> *The Female Spy*, p. 24

At the hospital, Emma worked closely with Chaplain Bee and his young wife, Kate. Kate had met her husband when Chaplain Bee took over pastorship of the church she attended with her parents in Flint, Michigan. Although the good Chaplain was at least ten years older than Kate, the two had fallen in love and married. Kate always called her husband "Reverend" or "dear." The men of the 2nd Michigan simply called him Chaplain Bee.

The good chaplain's primary duties were to counsel the troubled and sick, but he and Kate also wrote and read letters for the illiterate men and frequently took charge of the incoming and outgoing mail for the entire regiment.

Lively and pretty young Kate took an instant liking to the dedicated young male nurse she called "Frankie." At the height of the typhoid epidemic, Kate and Emma worked tirelessly side by side, carrying medicine and comfort to the afflicted men. It was good, useful work, and Emma was contented with it.

The heat was unbearable at times, only relieved by the frequent thunderstorms that swept through the Potomac Valley in the evenings. During one of these storms, Emma and Kate stood outside a hospital tent, holding down the ropes and tent poles so that the sick would be protected from the wind and rain.

"What drives you, Frankie," Kate had asked after the storm had passed and they were busy repairing the leaking tents and distributing rubber blankets.

"Answering the call seemed a good way to see the country. And a chance to be a part of something big, I suppose," said Emma. "And you, Mrs. B? You came here to be with Chaplain B, I suppose?" asked Emma.

"Well, yes, that too. But I think I would have come without Chaplain B, Frankie. Like him, I feel it is my *duty* to be here. Not duty to my country, but rather duty to the poor men here who will be risking their lives in the coming battles. I'm here because I'm supposed to be here, I guess. So are you, for your own reasons," said Kate.

But Emma wasn't so sure that Kate was totally correct in her assessment of Emma's situation. She thought about the tyrant father she had escaped, not once but twice now, and the adventure she hoped to find by joining the army. Though her satisfaction with her nursing responsibilities was real, at least one of Emma's reasons for joining the service was quite personal, having none of the higher calling to honor that drove Kate and Chaplain Bee.

Other soldiers she knew were driven by politics and love of country, and they volunteered to fight because they wished to abolish slavery and preserve the best government on earth. For these soldiers, the march to Washington had been a long but necessary trip on unwanted business. Emma had heard one volunteer explain it well. "Got to get this war over so's I kin get the hayin' done and cut the brush before the oats is ready." Many others were driven by a need to prove themselves on a field of battle, and they sought honor and glory through combat. But most, she knew, were like Emma herself, driven by self centeredness and hoping to get a break from the monotony of farm work or rote labor of their peacetime lives. They were in it for the adventure, the excitement, and the grand opportunity to see more of the world than their own corn fields. How much longer before this thing begins, Emma wondered as she drifted into sleep.

Emma's *journal:*

July 15, 1861
Marching orders received to-day--two days more, and the Army will be on its way.

Chapter 5
First Bull Run

Emma looked around her at the battlefield. The ground was crimson with blood.

Men bled.

They died.

Wounded horses screamed and thrashed.

Suddenly, Col. Cameron came dashing along the line.

"The rebels are in retreat," he shouted before he was shot through the heart. Colonel Cameron fell to the ground, dead.

Emma and Kate folded his arms across his breast, closed his eyes and left him, for Colonel Cameron had been misinformed. The Rebels were in pursuit.

On the hill overlooking the battlefield, the spectators suddenly began to run, leaving their picnics still spread out upon the ground.

The horses ran, pulling the empty buggies.

All at once, it seemed that everyone was running towards her.

They ran past her and she saw the Rebels coming.

Emma turned and ran, as the minie balls whizzed around her.

When she reached the turnpike, Emma joined others in the retreating Union Army. Some of the soldiers had thrown away their guns when they turned their backs on the enemy. Now, they walked slowly, their heads down and shoulders drooping; others ran frantically, afraid of what they had seen and done on this terrible, hot summer day.

Emma believed that sometimes it took great courage to run from an enemy. Running away from her father had been the most difficult thing she'd ever done. And today, they had no choice but to run from the advancing enemy. She quickened her pace.

And then the rain came, drenching the fugitives who were making their way back to the capital. Emma arrived at the field hospital in Centreville, where she was relieved to find Kate already taking care of the wounded in the shelter of an old stone house. As the casualties came in, they were sorted into three categories. The mortally wounded were given water, made comfortable and left alone. The slightly wounded reported to the dressing surgeon, who cleaned and bandaged the wounds and gave them opiates for pain. The most pitiful were the surgical cases, who lay in their own blood and gore awaiting the services of the surgeon, and most likely, amputation.

Emma was appalled at the scene of suffering before her. Minie balls left gaping wounds, taking clothing and dirt into flesh and bone. Most of the wounded suffered a raging thirst, and cries for water filled her ears. One wounded soldier, whose legs were both broken above the knees, cried out for water, thrashing his arms and torso, and Emma turned to help him. There were black circles around his mouth where powder had stained his face as he tore open cartridges with his teeth. Emma looked at his legs and saw that inflammation had already set in. Her eyes met Kate's as they held him down. Kate shook her head.

"Make him comfortable," the surgeon said, and then the poor fellow died and Emma was surprised that she was glad for him.

In the next bed, a gray-bearded soldier asked, "Do you think I'll die before morning?" Emma looked at the gaping hole in the man's side. The surgeon's attempt to staunch the flow of blood had failed, and the bed was soaked crimson. Emma took his hand and said, "I think so."

The old soldier smiled, and closed his eyes. "Then it is time for me to rest," he whispered, "for I have sent many Rebs to hell this day."

How easy it was to kill someone, and how hard it was to die, thought Emma as she held the canteen so the wounded man could drink.

"Does death not hold any terrors for you?" asked Emma.

"Oh no," he said, and opened his eyes and looked straight at her. "Soon I shall be asleep in Jesus."

Emma thought it strange that when the order to charge had been given, not one soldier had appeared to give the least thought to breaking God's commandment against killing.

Emma and Kate did what they could for the wounded and dying. Outside the stone house, stacks of dead bodies were piled high, with arms and legs thrown together in heaps. Emma was fetching more water from the well when a Union soldier rode into the front yard, shouting.

"Get out while you can, soldier," he said, reigning his horse to a stop. "The army has retreated. We are surrounded by Confederates!" He tied his horse to the fence and went into the stone house to tell the others.

Emma was stunned. Perhaps the soldier was wrong. She rushed up to the heights where the troops had camped at night. The place was deserted. Maybe they had changed their position. When she returned to the stone house, the chaplain and Kate were waiting for her, grim looks upon their weary faces.

"We have informed the wounded that the Rebels are coming. They understand that our army has left. There is no possibility of moving them," said Chaplain Bee.

Kate stood beside her husband, her black riding habit encrusted with the dried blood of the many wounded she and Emma had carried off the field that day.

"But what of the these men?" Emma asked, nodding her head towards the hospital. "We can't just leave them to the enemy."

"We must, Frankie," said Kate. "They cannot be moved, and our work now is in the hospital in Washington. Come with us now. Please, Frankie."

"No. I cannot, will not leave these wounded," Emma protested.

Kate walked to Emma and laid her hand upon her arm. "You can help more of our men and do more good if you escape capture, Frankie. The Rebels will care for our wounded. It is the able bodied soldier such as yourself who will feel the sting of the enemy," said Kate.

Emma looked at her friends' troubled faces and knew that they were right. For the second time that day, she must run away from the enemy.

"Leave me my horse, and I'll follow you soon," said Emma. She must go into the house once more, even at the risk of being taken prisoner.

Inside, the men were remarkably calm. Only the groans of the dying and a few calls for water could be heard. Emma filled the canteens and left them by the door, but as she turned to leave, a voice called her back.

"Nurse, please help me," said a young soldier wounded in the stomach who lay on some blankets near the door. She went to him and knelt beside him. It was then that Emma heard the unmistakable tramp of cavalry in the road, but she turned her full attention upon the wounded soldier.

"What can I do for you, friend?" she asked. The soldier opened his eyes, and pointed to a small package that lay beside him. With an effort, he said, "I want you to take that with you when you leave. Send it to my mother and write to her telling her how I was wounded." His eyes closed, and he signed to Emma to come nearer, and when she leaned over him, he touched a lock of his hair, then died.

Understanding his silent message, Emma cut off a lock of the boy's hair with her pocket knife and added it to the package to send to his mother. The boy at least had won a victory today, notwithstanding the defeat of the Federal army.

Emma stood and quickly left the building. Outside, she leapt upon the horse that Kate had left tied nearby and headed for the woods. If she was to escape, she dare not follow the main road.

Chapter 6
Waiting for Marching Orders

Emma rode through the wet night until she reached Alexandria, where she finally stopped to bathe and rest at a hotel. That night, she dreamed that she was running away as the Rebels gave chase screeching the blood chilling yell that she had heard on the battlefield of Bull Run. In her nightmare, the enemy had her father's face.

The next morning Emma mailed the dead soldier's package to his mother. Two days later, a refreshed "Frank Thompson" rejoined "his" regiment in Washington.

The capital was in despair, and the soldiers were downcast as newspapers and telegraphs spread the news of the disaster throughout the country and beyond.

Setback at Bull Run
Manassas, Virginia
July 21, 1861

The first thrust by Union forces toward the Confederate capital of Richmond has been repulsed. The Union army of 34,000 men under Brigadier General Irvin McDowell met the Confederate army led by General Pierre Beauregard that was waiting behind a creek called Bull Run, three miles from Centreville, Virginia. Although regiments went into battle piecemeal, at first it looked as though the Union forces would win. When fresh Confederate reinforcements arrived, these brigades broke through the battle-weary Union forces.

The Union retreat was chaotic, taking noncombatant spectators by surprise, and soon turned into a

*rout that did not stop until the Union troops returned
to Washington.*

The terrible march through the rain and mud from Bull
Run to Washington did more toward filling the hospitals than
did the battle itself. Typhoid, dysentery and measles raged
among the soldiers, and Emma was busy nursing the sick
and wounded. She found her friend Kate in the hospital
suffering from dysentery, attended by her husband, the
sympathetic and energetic Chaplain.

From Emma's *Memoirs:*

> *Oh, what an amount of suffering I am called to
> witness every hour and every moment. There is
> no cessation, and yet it is strange that the sight
> of all this suffering and death does not affect me
> more. I am simply eyes, ears, hands and feet. It
> does seem as if there is a sort of stoicism grant-
> ed for such occasions. There are great, strong
> men dying all around me, and while I write
> there are three being carried past the window to
> the dead room. This is an excellent hospital--
> everything is kept in good order, and the medi-
> cal officers are skillful, kind and attentive.*
> > *The Female Spy,* p. 58

The weary weeks passed as Emma continued to work day
and night at the hospital. Soon, Kate recovered and resumed
her working partnership with young "Frankie," and Emma
was glad for the female companionship since when she was
in camp with the men, she had to be most careful to remain
aloof lest her disguise be uncovered. If Kate had any

suspicions about "Frankie's" identity, she kept them to herself.

As the winter months passed, the Union Army, now recovered from the disaster of Bull Run, became restless from the long period of inactivity. They were ready for another battle. At the hospital, Emma endeared herself to the sick and wounded men, amusing them with her gift of mimicry. A lisp, a dialect, a swagger--once observed, Emma could imitate it perfectly. Emma used her gift generously, for she found that laughter was sometimes a more effective medicine that the potions dispensed by the surgeons.

During this time of waiting, camp life was filled with routine busyness, but the waiting for marching orders seemed intolerable. Spring arrived, and the Army of 250,000 soldiers remained immobile.

But for Emma, the drum and bugle calls divided life into neat, safe compartments. Her life assumed a pattern that she found comforting in its routine dependability. But she soon grew restless with boredom.

From Emma's *Memoirs:*

> *At sunrise reveille beats, drum echoing to drum until the entire encampment is astir, and busy as a bee-hive. Roll-call immediately follows, which brings every man to his place in the ranks, to answer to his name. An hour later breakfast call is sounded by fife and drum, and the company cooks, who are detailed for that purpose, deal out the rations to the men as they sit or stand around the cook's quarters.*
>
> *At half-past seven o'clock sick call announces to surgeons and patients that they are expected to appear at the dispensing tent--if able to go there. Then comes a general examination of tongues and pulses, and a*

liberal distribution of quinine and blue pills, and sometimes a little eau de vie to wash down the bitter drugs.

Guard mounting at eight. . . At nine o'clock the music sounds for company drill, which drill lasts an hour and a half. The bugle announces dinner at one o'clock.

At three in the afternoon battalion drill commences, which occupies an hour. At half past four is heard the first call for evening parade, and at five o'clock comes off the great display of the day--dress parade.

Supper at six, tattoo at half past eight, and roll call again at nine; immediately after which comes "taps" on the drum, which means "lights out."
The Female Spy, pp. 282-3

The monotony of camp life began to change when skirmishing broke out between the Union and Confederate pickets, those soldiers who were posted ahead of the armies to guard against surprise attacks. One day, Emma and Kate rode out towards Munson's Hill to tend to the wounded Federal skirmishers. Kate had shortened her black cloth riding habit to walking length. Emma, dressed in Union uniform, carried a canteen of water swung over one shoulder and a flask of brandy over the other. A haversack with provisions, lint, bandages and adhesive plaster hung by her side.

They heard the guns before they saw the pickets. "Look there," said Emma pointing to the west as they crested a knoll that allowed them to see the picket lines of both armies. The pickets were posted in plain sight of each other, separated by a cornfield and a peach orchard that offered little protection from the flying minie balls.

"Captain said truce flags had been sent in on both sides. Doesn't look like either side's willing to stop, even so. Better leave the horses here," said Kate.

Emma and Kate rode to the clump of trees, dismounted and hitched the horses, following the tree line on foot towards the Federal rifle pit. Minie balls whizzed above them when the Confederates caught sight of them, so they dropped to their hands and knees and scrambled towards the safety of their own picket line. Once, a minie ball whizzed so close to Emma's ear, she felt the movement of air as it passed, and a split second later heard the sound of its firing. She tasted blood, and for a moment thought she was wounded, but then realized she had merely bitten her tongue. She turned to see if Kate was behind her and was relieved to see that she was still there.

"Keep going, Frankie. Hurry," Kate urged.

Another minie ball whizzed by, this time knocking off Emma's hat. The sounds of the minie balls differed depending on how close they came to something solid. One sounded like a kitten's meow as it whistled by Emma's ear. Another whizzed by, wailing like the Canadian winter wind, and the ball slammed into the earth in front of her.

Emma crouched lower, still moving forward, looking at the ground. The sound of blood pounded in her ears and her heart hammered wildly in her chest. Emma saw things she had never noticed before--the green of new grass shoots pushing through the brown blades, the smell of the damp wool of her trousers, the feel of the soft earth beneath her hands and knees. Beyond the gun fire, she thought she could hear a hawk calling as it circled its prey. All her senses seemed to be heightened, and she wondered if this was a sign that she was to die in this meadow, not in the heat of battle, after all, but because a bored soldier had ignored an order for truce.

Suddenly Emma realized that she had finally reached the picket line, and she scrambled into the rifle pit with Kate right behind her. They tended the wounded man as best they could, working long after the skirmishing stopped, and the air grew silent as shadows deepened into an inky moonlit night. At last, under cover of darkness, Emma and Kate made their way back to their horses.

"Why did they fire on us when flags of truce were displayed on both sides?" asked Emma. "Useless butchery is what I call it."

"Stress of war seems to turn some men either of two ways," observed Kate, as they were riding back to camp. "Cowards or killers." Emma thought about the retreat at Bull Run, and nodded.

"Either way, it's a sickness. Either way, hope they can get over it once the war's done," said Emma. But when they returned to camp, Emma learned that the real fighting was about to begin.

Address of General McClellan to the Union Army:

For a long time I have kept you inactive, but not without a purpose. You were to be disciplined, armed and instructed. The formidable artillery you now have had to be created. Other armies were to move and accomplish certain results. I have held you back that you might give the death-blow to the rebellion that has distracted our once happy country. The patience you have shown, and your confidence in your General, are worth a dozen victories. These preliminary results are now accomplished. I feel that the patient labors of many months have produced their fruit. The army of the Potomac is now a real army, magnificent in material, admirable in discipline and instruction, excellently equipped and armed. Your commanders are all that I could wish. The moment for action has arrived, and I know that I can trust in you to save our country. The period of inaction has passed. I will bring you now face to face with the Rebels, and only pray that God may defend the right.

The Female Spy, p. 65

Emma Edmonds, a.k.a. Frank Thompson, once again felt charged with the spirit of high adventure. At last the war was about to begin.

Chapter 7
A Surprise for Emma

The army arrived at Fortress Monroe in a drenching rain and pitched their tents in the mud. The cold rain lasted for several more days, bringing with it fever and ague that swept the camp. This time, Emma did not escape the epidemic. She suffered alone in her tent, alternately roasting and shivering, refusing the attention of everyone, even Kate and Chaplain Bee. One day Kate stopped by Emma's tent with quinine and whiskey to treat the fever.

"You should be in the hospital with the rest of the sick boys, Frankie," Kate pleaded. So many of the soldiers were suffering from the same malaria fevers as Emma.

"No need for that. I'm a nurse. Can care for myself here just as well," said Emma as she gratefully accepted the cup of whiskey from her friend.

"At least let me help you bathe while I'm here," Kate persisted.

"Heat me some water and leave. Go help those who need you," said Emma abruptly, and turned her back on Kate, feeling guilty for refusing her friend's kindness. Emma trusted Kate to be what she seemed, but what deception was Emma perpetrating on Kate, her dearest friend in all the world?

After Kate left, Emma undressed and washed her thin, fever-racked body.

By the end of the week Emma's fever had left, but the illness left her unsteady and weak, unable to be of much help in nursing others. The rainy weather continued, and cast a foul temper upon the entire camp, even those lucky enough to stay healthy. Once again, the army awaited marching orders. Emma, sick in body and spirit, grew ever more despondent with the wait. Then one day she received a most unexpected surprise.

"There's a box at the express office for you," said Chaplain Bee one morning as he was distributing the mail to the men. "Kate's gone to fetch it for you."

"What kind of box? Is it from my mother in Canada?" asked Emma. Emma had not heard from her mother since the letter she had received asking her to give up the army and come home. Nor had Emma written to her mother.

"Don't know who it's from, Frankie, but this letter came with it," said the Chaplain, and he handed her the envelope.

Emma's hands shook as she unfolded the sheets of paper.

Dear Private Thompson,

I learned of your address through another whose son also died at the battle of Bull Run. I send you this donation in token of my respect and esteem, and for my gratitude to you in sending me my beloved son's belongings after that same battle. The love and prayers of a bereaved mother will follow you all through the journey of your life.

Emma remembered the boy who lay dying on the floor of the old stone house at Centreville. His mother must have loved him very much to have tracked down "Frank Thompson." Just then Kate came, carrying the package.

"For you, Frankie," said Kate, setting the box at Emma's feet.

"It is from the mother of a boy who died at Bull Run. You must stay and help me open it. You certainly have a right to it. You did as much as I did for those poor boys," said Emma.

With the sun warm on their backs, Emma and Kate tore open the box, and marveled over the exquisite delights inside. Emma wrote about the box and its contents in her journal that afternoon:

From Emma's *Memoirs*:

First came a beautiful silk and rubber reversible cloak, which could be folded into such a small compass that it could be put into an ordinary sized pocket, and a pair of rubber boots. Then came a splendid silver-mounted revolver belt and miniature cartridge box...in the bottom, stowed away in one corner, two bottles of the best currant wine, a nice jar of jelly, and a large loaf of cake, frosted and mottoed in fine style. This cake was certainly a great curiosity. It was a three-story cake, with three doors made to slide back by gently pulling a bell-handle which was made of rosettes of red, white and blue ribbon. To the first bell-cord was attached a splendid gold ring, to the second a ten dollar gold piece, and to the third and last a small sized hunting cased gold watch and chain. At such revelations I began to feel as if my humble tent had become an enchanted palace, and that all I should have to do in future would be to rub that mysterious ring, and the genii would appear, ready to supply all my wants.
The Female Spy, pp. 78-79

News of the wonderful box spread throughout the camp, and by evening, many had come to see and, hopefully, share the spoils. Young "Frankie" who liked to keep to "himself," suddenly was the center of attention. Kate helped cut the cake and pour the wine and the party grew cheerfully rowdy. Some of the men brought out their own gifts from home, bread and crackers, cakes and jams.

Late into the evening, when the food and wine was finally finished, Emma had another surprise that eclipsed the pleasure she took in her gifts.

"Frankie! Look who I've just met! One of your fellow countrymen. And a fine fellow he is too. I told him he just must meet you," said Kate.

Emma saw that the young man wore the uniform of a Lieutenant of the Seventy-Ninth New York Volunteer Infantry Regiment. He walked towards her with a swagger she recognized. Suddenly, bees swarmed in her belly, and she had a sour taste in her mouth, and she felt the same fear grip her that she felt when she and Kate were crawling to safety from the sniper fire. Kate was saying something to her. Emma saw Kate's lips move but her words buzzed meaninglessly in Emma's ears. Now the young man was saying something, and Emma tried to respond but her greeting died in her throat as her eyes met those of her old friend, James Vesey.

Chapter 8
An Idea Worth Dying For

E mma felt dizzy. Would her old friend recognize her, and if so, would he give away her secret? From the shadow of her hat pulled low over her forehead, Emma looked at the changes that five years had wrought in the face of her beloved James as he stood talking to Kate. James' face was thinner, his body lean and fit. He had grown at least six inches since their parting, but then surely she had changed some too in the years since he had last seen her.

Kate was showing James the contents of the box, and when Emma recovered a bit, she joined them beside the campfire.

"Sorry, sir, to be so abrupt. Too much celebrating tonight made me queasy," said Emma.

"Our Frankie has been quite ill, Lieutenant," Kate added.

"I quite understand," said James. He stepped towards her and smiled. Emma adjusted her hat and took a step backward into the flickering shadows cast by the campfire.

"Perhaps when you are feeling up to it, you could stop by my quarters so we can discuss our Canadian roots. No doubt, we have some friends in common," said James.

"Of course, sir," said Emma.

The next evening as soon as it grew dark, Emma made her way to Lieutenant James Vesey's quarters.

"Always glad to meet up with another Canadian," said James. "What province do you hail from?"

"Nova Scotia," Emma lied, "And you?"

"New Brunswick is my home, though I've not been back since my parents died. Still have the farm there, though, and I might go back to it after the war's done," said James. "What business is your family in, Private Thompson?"

"My family's long worked in the millinery trade," said Emma. A half truth at best, but Emma felt she had better stick to what she knew and could talk about.

The conversation was interrupted by tattoo calling some of the men to drill. James pulled out his pocket watch and flipped open the lid.

"A fine timepiece, Lieutenant," said Emma, recognizing the same watch James had carried with him when they were children together.

"A gift from my mother many years ago, Private. And I had hoped to give it to my sweetheart in Canada, but I left before I got a chance," said James.

A sweetheart in Canada, probably someone she knew. She wondered if it was Sallie MacGregor, the Magaguadavic girl rumored to be sweet on James so many years ago.

"Here, take a look at the filigree on the case. My mother had it specially engraved." James took the watch from its chain and handed it to Emma. She opened the lid and looked at the familiar dial. The watch was warm in her hand and in the slanting afternoon light, the glass reflected back another face--her own, and she barely recognized herself. She saw a young man with a long straight nose and piercing eyes set in a face turned bronze and hard from long marching and drilling in the harsh outdoor weather. She snapped the lid closed and handed the watch back to James.

"Very fine timepiece. You can look up your sweetheart after the war. I'm sure she'll take the watch then. It's a beauty," she said.

"What about you. You married?" asked James.

"Na, I'm just nineteen. Too young," said Emma.

"At least you won't leave a widow. Too bad though. A wife or a sweetheart waiting helps a man hold on during war," said James.

"Yes," she murmured. Emma remembered all the men who lay dying after the battle of Bull Run. So many of the mortally wounded had the names of their sweethearts on their lips as they breathed their last.

One night a few days later, Emma was startled out of a deep sleep by shouting.

"Glory! Glory to God!"

Emma crawled out of her pup tent and found that the whole camp was awake, with everyone rushing around trying to find out the cause of the excitement. In the midst of the sleepy soldiers was a band of about forty men, women and children, most black as midnight, all huddled together in a group, praying and shouting praises to God, arms held high. One man dropped to his knees and clasped his hands in prayer as he wept. Two soldiers came with bread and coffee and the refugees began to eat.

Emma stared at the ragged looking group. It was her first look at people of color. She had heard Chaplain Bee and Kate talk about the evils of slavery, but until now she never understood who was at stake. Now she looked upon the happy group of black faces with curiosity.

Among the throng of sleepy soldiers surrounding the refugees, was James, and Emma made her way towards him. Just as Emma joined him, the refugees began singing and dancing, encouraged by the men surrounding them.

"These are former slaves, who've escaped their bondage. That makes them contraband," said James. "They said they'd been sold down south to prevent them from running to the protection of the Union. They got to us anyway."

When things had settled down a bit, Chaplain Bee led some hymns that Emma knew by heart, but the contraband sang other songs she did not recognize, and Emma was swept up by the rhythm of their voices:

We'll fight for liberty,
We'll fight for liberty,
We'll fight for liberty,
When de Lord will call us home.
   And it won't be long,
   And it won't be long,
   And it won't be long,
When de Lord will call us home.

The wild, sad strains of the old melody stirred Emma, though the words seemed inspired by recent events. James told her that several Negroes had been thrown in jail in South Carolina for singing the spiritual.

"How do you feel about slavery?" James asked Emma. Growing up in Canada, Emma hadn't really had occasion to consider the question in any real sense, and neither, she thought, had James. But the idea of slavery, of one human owning another, seemed evil to her. Emma knew she could never articulate her feelings without giving up her disguise to this friend beside her who once knew her so well, so she just shrugged.

"I do not believe in it," she said simply.

"Slavery's just one issue dividing this country, Frankie. But it's the reason I joined this war. Look at those people over there," he said, pointing to three of the contraband, apparently family members, who were being served coffee and bread. The young man and two children were light skinned, and their brown hair gleamed in the firelight. "When I look at those people, I think of the slave owner. Why should these people be kept as slaves while four or five of his other children are kept as pampered pets?"

Emma thought about the factories she had seen in Lowell, Massachusetts, and of the poor people who worked in them. She had thought at the time that the factory was hell on earth, probably worse than slavery, but she couldn't be sure.

"Lots of ways to own people, and slavery is one of the worst, it seems to me," said Emma. "Owning another person just isn't right, in the north or in the south. Shouldn't take a war to figure that out."

"Then why are you fighting?" James asked and turned to face her. "This isn't your country, so you can't be all that patriotic about saving the Union."

Emma turned away from him and watched as the refugees were given dry clothing and refreshments. One of the reasons she had come to this war was to escape a domineering father, a parent who would make of her a slave of yet another kind than the ragged group of people before her. If the truth be known, she was more afraid of that bondage than of fighting in any battle. But of course, she couldn't tell that to James without giving herself away. So she said nothing and continued to watch the contraband.

"When I watch them, I see Uncle Tom, Quimbo, Sambo, Chloe and Eliza from *Uncle Tom's Cabin*, and I'm moved to help end all slavery," said James as the rowdy meeting finally came to an end. "Freedom. Now there's an idea worth dying for. It's what brought me to this army. This army is going to alter the course of history, Frankie. And you and me are going to be a part of it."

Emma slept very little that night, mulling over James' words. Before daybreak, she rose to write in her journal.

From Emma's *Memoirs:*

> *Visited the contraband to-day, and was much pleased with their cheerful, happy appearance... Almost all with whom I conversed to-day were praying men and women. Oh, how I should like to teach these people! They seem so anxious for instruction, I know they would learn quickly... There is a family here, all of whom have blue eyes, light hair, fair skin and rosy cheeks; yet they are contraband, and have been slaves. But why should blue eyes and golden hair be the distinction between bond and free?*
>
> *The Female Spy*, p. 72-3

Emma didn't have long to ponder the injustice of slavery, for the very next day the army received marching orders. "On to Richmond" once more resounded throughout the camp, and the army prepared to move toward Yorktown.

Chapter 9
Two Shootings

The twenty-three mile march from Hampton to York-town was a miserable one. The cold spring rain pelted the marchers and turned the road to muck. Emma sank to her ankles in the mud as she trudged, and her shoes made strange sucking sounds as she pulled her feet out. Like the others who marched, Emma was loaded down with a haversack, cartridge box, bayonet, cap box, blanket, canteen and a knapsack with her personal belongings. The equipment weighed almost half of what Emma weighed alone. As the army moved, the route became littered with heavier and excess baggage items, including blankets, clothes, even Bibles and precious mementos from home if the soldier was desperately tired. Human litter that could be replaced at a later time was scattered like rubbish.

Mules and horses became hopelessly mired in the mud and had to be shot. The trials of the march hardened and soured many of the men, but Emma kept up her spirit in the cheerful company of Kate and Chaplain Bee, and of course, when she could manage to see him, Lieutenant James Vesey.

The army set up their tents in the mud several miles outside Yorktown, and once more settled down to wait. McClellan assured his army that there would soon be a great decisive battle. In the meantime, there was little to do and Emma grew bored. When she was not at her nursing duties, she read. There was ample reading material circulating among the men, and always a supply of newspapers brought into camp once a week by a sutler from Washington. The little man with the oily hair and rotten teeth set up his tent near headquarters where he would be easily accessible to the soldiers who wanted to purchase stationery, tobacco, reading material, and sometimes even whiskey, at exorbitant prices. Emma thought him unscrupulous and carefully counted her change each time she bought a newspaper. Once when Emma had protested the high cost of his goods, he had scoffed at her.

"Hoch! What do a young snot like you, without a whiska on your face, know about the cost of provisions. I should call you little woman instead of soldier," sneered the sutler, showing his corn kernel teeth. Emma had been chilled to think that her disguise might be uncovered by such a scoundrel. From that time on, Emma avoided him when she could and borrowed newspapers instead of purchasing them from the sutler.

It was during this time of waiting that Emma found she had another skill besides nursing, which quickly endeared "Frankie" to the men of the 2nd Michigan as they waited for the great battle to come. She could write interesting letters to people she had never even met.

To while away the time, many soldiers wrote lengthy letters home to their families. Some of the men were completely illiterate, and so they had to dictate their letters to someone else to transcribe for them. Accustomed to transcribing letters from the hospital wounded as they recuperated, "Frankie" now volunteered to help the soldiers in camp write letters.

She sat with pencil in hand as a stuttering youth uttered his awkward message:

Dear Ma and Pa. I am good. Hope you are too. It rained most of last week, and my shoes got ruined, but I think I can patch them up to last for a while longer if I can get some leather. Don't worry about me. Frank Thompson is helping me with this letter. Hello to everyone at home. Love, Oliver.

Emma listened to the soldier's words and her pencil flew across the page as she "flowered up" his message:

Dearest mother and father. Although last week's march through the mud and rain was almost too much to endure, please be assured that I am healthy and well. My parents raised a sturdy boy. The countryside is glorious, and camp life is tolerable as we await the opportunity to engage the enemy and end the rebellion once and for all. Please convey my love and best wishes to friends and relatives when they ask about me. I miss you very much, but am confident that this business will soon be over and I will be home in the bosom of my family once again. Love, Oliver. P.S. If you can manage it, could you please send me some shoes.

One day, James asked "Frankie" to accompany him on a ride to see the reconnaissance balloons. They saddled their horses and left the camp just as the sun came up on what promised to be a warm clear day.

It felt good to be riding across the countryside with James just as they had done as children. Emma looked up at the cloudless sky and felt the warmth of the early morning sun on her face. She smelled the rich aroma of newly plowed earth as it dried out in the April sun. A flock of geese trumpeted over their heads. It was hard to believe that such trouble divided a land so lovely, Emma thought.

There was no telling what made one moment more special than any other, but Emma knew that this morning would stay in her memory forever. The beauty of the day would be captured in her mind's eye like the photographs of loved ones that some soldiers brought to war with them, except that Emma's memory carried more than a vision.

"Early morning's generally the best time of day for aerial missions, cause the smoke from the evening campfires has cleared," explained James as they rode to the field station of the U.S. Balloon corps. "From the balloons, our men can see a good distance in every direction. They can get a pretty good idea of all the enemy positions."

The early morning mist cleared, revealing a scene of intense activity. Emma and James rode into the clearing just in time to watch the inflation of one of the three reconnaissance balloons, the Intrepid. Men poured containers of sulfuric acid into vats filled with iron fillings. This mixture created hydrogen that was pumped through hoses into the huge balloon.

Thirty men held ropes to keep the balloon anchored, while two men climbed into the wicker passenger basket. Emma and James were silent as the balloon rose majestically and floated off over the landscape.

"I should think they could see all the way to Canada from up there," said Emma, as the balloon drifted out of sight.

James laughed. "Fifteen miles in each direction on a clear day--enough to see the enemy positions, but not all the way to Canada," he said.

"Even if the observers don't see anything, I should think the balloons would be worth all they cost just because they make the enemy nervous," said Emma. "I should like to be in that wicker basket myself, suspended between heaven and earth."

James watched the balloon's ascension and then said, "I suspect that gathering intelligence from a balloon is not as leisurely as it appears, Frankie. Accidents happen. One time a reconnaissance balloon nearly landed in the enemy camp. Another time, a balloon landed in the Potomac and the observers nearly drowned. Dangerous business, spying from a balloon."

"Still,"Emma mused, "I should like to try it. I've seen death and I am not afraid of it. Besides, 'a wean that's born to be hung 'll ne'er be droon'd'," she said, slipping easily into the Scottish accent of her childhood pastor. Too late, she realized her slip. James regarded her closely, but said nothing.

The army remained in camp while McClellan collected information on the enemy's position. Emma, like the other soldiers, once again grew restless with waiting. Food was scarce, and the army routinely sent out "foragers" to scout the surrounding countryside in search of fresh food to supplement their rations. One bright morning, "Frankie" volunteered for one of these missions that she and Kate jokingly referred to as "catering business."

"We need eggs, butter and milk for the hospital," said Kate, as she helped Emma to saddle up Emma's horse, Rebel. The animal had been requisitioned to her by the chief of surgery so that she could fetch provisions from the better stocked hospitals in Washington D. C. The sturdy mare had once belonged to a cavalry officer, who claimed the animal bit him on the arm because the officer blew cigar smoke in the animal's face. The bite had caused a nasty infection that put an end to the officer's cavalry career. He named the horse Rebel, and gave her to the chief of surgery. Now in Emma's care, Rebel led a pampered life, subsisting on a diet of oats and cigar butts.

"Report says that the farmhouse three miles back on Hampton Road is well supplied with fresh provisions. I'll be back with the supplies before dark," promised Emma, and she mounted Rebel and cantered off briskly.

About three miles down the road, Emma came to a gate which opened into a dirt lane leading directly to an isolated farmhouse. It was a large, well kept, two-story structure, with immense chimneys built on the outside in the style of so many houses in Virginia. Unlike many of the farms in this part of enemy territory, the house and barn appeared to be in good condition. The fields were not plowed, but two cows and a horse were grazing in a nearby pasture, and chickens were scurrying about the yard.

Emma rode up to the house and dismounted, hitching Rebel to a post near the porch. Only a screened door separated Emma from the house, and she saw that most of the windows had been thrown open to the fresh spring breezes.

"To what fortunate circumstance am I to attribute the pleasure of this unexpected call?" queried a woman's voice from the depths of the house. The screen kept the woman from Emma's view.

"I've come to procure provisions for the Union Army. I mean to pay for whatever you can spare," said Emma.

The screen door was opened by a tall, beautiful woman. The woman's pale complexion was in contrast with her black mourning dress.

"Won't you come in and rest while I see what we have," said the elegant woman, and she led Emma into a small sitting room at the rear of the house.

"You can sit here and wait," said the woman. Although she appeared outwardly calm and charming, Emma felt suddenly uncomfortable for some reason. She watched the woman closely. Emma saw beads of perspiration on the woman's upper lip even though the room was cool from the breezes that swept through the room from the open window. And though she smiled at Emma, there was a wild, desperate look in her eyes as she showed Emma to a chair and invited her to sit down to wait while she gathered the provisions. Emma refused the seat and moved closer to the window where she had a view of the road and her horse.

"Thank you, ma'am, but I shall accompany you, if you don't mind. Perhaps I can be of some assistance in packing the provisions," said Emma.

"Of course. I will certainly cooperate in the best interest of my country," said the woman. Her voice, though soft and polite, confused Emma momentarily. Emma detected something else in that low pitched drawl. The woman's fingers flickered nervously over the front of her jet black skirt and her eyes were hard. Emma tensed, only momentarily taking her eyes off the woman as she slowly gathered eggs and milk from her pantry.

With trembling fingers, the woman packed butter and apples together into a small wicker basket. Emma was good at dissembling and she recognized the ruse in this woman. Something was not as it seemed.

"Are things ready now? If so, I must be moving along," said Emma, as she took the basket from her.

"I did not know that you were in a hurry. I am waiting for my boys to come and catch some chickens for you, if you can spare the time, that is," said the woman.

"And pray, madam, where are your boys," Emma asked her, still moving towards the door.

"They aren't far from here," was her reply, her voice trembling. Emma grew suddenly fearful. Supposing that her boys were Rebel sympathizers, and Emma was all alone.

"I thank you for what you have given me, but I must be on my way now," said Emma, and she held out a greenback to the woman as payment for the food.

The woman drew back at Emma's outstretched hand. "Oh no, it is no consequence about the pay. You take the food and do with it as you will," she said.

Emma thanked her and stepped out onto the porch with the basket in hand, grateful for the fresh air and sunshine that brought back a feeling of normalcy once again.

Emma placed the basket on top of the hitching post, untied Rebel and took her seat atop the horse. Just as she was reaching for the basket, Emma felt the bullet whiz past her face. A split second later she heard the discharge. Dropping the basket, Emma whirled Rebel around to see the woman in black as she was aiming to fire the second time. Instinctively, Emma crouched low over Rebel's neck and the ball passed harmlessly over her head.

Emma reached for her own revolver just as the woman aimed a third time. Emma took deliberate aim at the woman's hand and pulled the trigger. With a shriek that ended in a sob, the woman dropped to the porch floor in a black heap, holding out her left hand. A bullet had passed neatly though her palm.

"Don't shoot! Don't shoot me again," the woman sobbed.

Emma picked up the woman's pistol from where she had dropped it and shoved it into her belt, and then she pointed her own revolver at the woman who lay at her feet. Emma hoped that the gunshots and screaming hadn't alarmed anyone within calling distance. All her senses were acute. She scanned the landscape for any sign of movement.

"Where are your boys?" Emma shouted. "Where are they?"

The woman was still sobbing noiselessly, her shoulders shaking. She covered her face with her hands, the bloodied one leaving streaks of red that blended with her tears.

"My boys are behind the house," the woman sobbed, and Emma, startled at the revelation, whirled around and pointed her revolver towards the house. Surely she could not get away if the woman's sons were working behind the house. They should have heard the shots.

"Behind the house, in the ground. My boys are all dead,"
said the woman.

Emma helped the woman to her feet and into the house,
where she washed the wound and bandaged it.

The woman was finally calm, as though the shooting had
released some violent demon out of her. She said her name
was Nellie and her boys were actually her husband, father
and two brothers, all sharpshooters in the Rebel army, and
the first to fall in battle at Manassas.

"You're very kind. You have a gentle touch for a man,"
said the woman when Emma had finished dressing the
wound.

"I am a nurse. Most of us are men but there are a few
women nurses who follow the camp. I hope it can be said
that all of us are gentle," said Emma.

"You are the first Yankee that I have seen since I got the
news about my boys," said Nellie. "Now I am all alone."

"You'll see many more Yankees in the days to come. Our
camp is nearby," said Emma as she rose to leave. Nellie
reached out and grasped Emma's arm.

"I want you to take me with you. I have nothing to stay
here for," said Nellie.

"But what will you do with the Federal army, Nellie?
They are your sworn enemy. Just an hour ago, you would
have murdered me to prove it," said Emma.

"I'm sorry I shot at you. I want to make it up to you. I
can work beside you and help care for the wounded and
sick," said Nellie.

"Then why don't you volunteer for the Rebel army?
They'll have plenty of wounded as soon as this war heats
up," said Emma.

Nellie sighed, and let go of Emma's arm. "I leave it to you men to fight the wars," said Nellie. "On both sides, it's women like me that are left to accept defeat. What difference does it make then which side I'm on?"

In the end, Emma took Nellie back with her and placed her in the care of the army surgeon, who never could solve the mystery of Nellie's gunshot wound. Nellie only said that she was shot by a Yankee.

From Emma's *Memoirs:*

> *The next day she [Nellie] returned to her house in an ambulance, accompanied by a hospital steward, and brought away everything which could be made use of in the hospitals, and so took up her abode with us...*
> *As soon as she was well enough to act in the capacity of nurse she commenced in good earnest, and became one of the most faithful and efficient nurses in the army of the Potomac.*
> *The Female Spy*, p. 96-97

Emma soon began to be restless with her hospital duties and the strain of keeping her false identity. With the army stalled on the Peninsular, there was little to break the monotony of routine. Emma, still weak from her bout with malaria, began to think about giving up her ruse. With no one else to talk to about her dilemma, Emma confided in her journal:

> *Am considering going immediately to the general's headquarters and admit that I am not Franklin Thompson, but am instead Sarah Emma Edmonds from New Brunswick, Canada. Dismissal from the army would be my lot, and I can't say that I wouldn't welcome it at*

this time. Perhaps I should go back to Moncton and stay with Annie and wait for James. I long to become Emma once more.

Then, before she could act on her decision, Emma returned one afternoon from another foraging expedition and found the camp nearly deserted. An unusual silence pervaded, and as Emma made her way with the provisions to the hospital, she saw a procession of soldiers slowly winding their way from a fresh grave in a nearby orchard. A chill gripped Emma, worse than any cold she had felt even when she lay suffering from malaria. The line of soldiers approached Emma as she watched their long measured tread, their faces sad.

"Whose burial?" Emma asked the first soldier in line.

"Lieutenant James Vesey," was the reply.

Chapter 10
Where Duty Calls

Emma sat on a stump outside her tent, tearless and silent, but her thoughts raged within. *My friend, James! You died and I was not with you. It can't be true! It must be someone else!*

Kate and Chaplain Bee came to her as she sat in her confusion and despair.

"Frankie, dear," said Kate, laying a hand on Emma's shoulder. Emma looked into her friend's sad eyes, and sobbed, not caring for once that her tears were out of character of the tough "Frankie."

"Your friend was sent to carry an order from headquarters to the picket line, Frankie. An enemy minie ball struck him in the head," said Kate.

Emma wept.

"He was brought to the hospital, Frankie. I cared for him until he died. He asked me to give this to you," said Kate, and she held out James' gold watch. When Emma did not take it, Kate reached for her hand and placed the watch and chain into her palm. Kate and Chaplain Bee left her to mourn alone.

Night came at last, but Emma could not sleep. She tried to imagine her childhood friend dead and could not. She lay awake for hours, hearing James' voice, seeing James' face. They had buried him, and she had not seen him, and an odd feeling of hate for his killer surged through her, surprising her in its intensity. Quietly, she slipped from the tent. The cool night air felt soothing on her face. With a hasty word of explanation to the camp guard, she made her way through the midnight gloom to the orchard and was soon beside James' grave.

The smell of the freshly turned earth mingled with the scent of the fruit tree blossoms. Emma sat upon the grave, her head in her hands. James, her friend, and yes, her sweetheart, now gone, not in the heat of battle, but by the chance of a lone minie ball fired deliberately by the enemy. This war with its killing and sickness and misery was terrible, and she hoped it would soon end. Another kind of war now raged inside Emma and it terrified her. Now she understood better why Nellie had fired on her that day. Hate for the murderer of her loved ones had driven Nellie to attempt murder. And now Emma burned with hatred for the unseen Rebel who had taken James' life.

Emma remembered a Yankee boy who had fired upon the advancing Rebels at the battle of Bull Run. The boy's father had been wounded as father and son fought side by side. When his father fell, the boy picked up the father's musket and cartridge box and took deliberate aim at one Rebel after another, saying "May God have mercy upon your miserable soul," as he sent the bullets into the hearts of his enemies. At the time, Emma had thought the effort pathetic. Now she thought it noble.

The night air was growing damp, and Emma wrapped her arms around her body underneath her coat, and as she did so her fingers brushed the smooth, cool metal of James' watch. She withdrew it and held it in her fist, feeling the metal grow warm in her touch and she pressed it to her lips. James' watch--now hers. He had wanted her to have it, Kate said. She turned the watch over in her palm and opened the front cover and looked at the timepiece. Then she snapped it shut and opened the back cover, and inside was a picture of James' mother and a four leaf clover, dry and brittle but still green. Emma sighed and snapped the cover shut. *Didn't bring you much luck after all, did it my friend,* she thought.

In the week that followed James' death, a deep depression settled over Emma. Her whole life was a sham. She had deceived her best friend James, the only person to ever truly understand her. And she continued to deceive those who cared about her, including Nellie and Kate and Chaplain Bee. She grew increasingly discontent with military life.

One evening, Emma sought out Kate and Chaplain Bee. She found them resting in their tent, looking weary and grim after their shift at the hospital.

"You look tired, friends. I, too, am worn out. Worn out, pure and simple. I just don't have the enthusiasm for nursing anymore," Emma began.

"You want to leave your duties at the hospital then?" asked Kate.

"It's more than that. I have deceived you both, my dear friends, for too long. I must ask you to help me now, so that I can be myself," said Emma, screwing up her courage.

"If it's reassignment you need to restore you to your former health and good spirits, I would be happy to intercede, Frankie. In fact, just this morning I learned of a situation that I could get for you immediately," said the Chaplain.

"It's not just my health, Chaplain. I'm not what I seem," Emma continued, but the chaplain had turned aside and was busy rummaging through his haversack. He pulled out a folded newspaper and handed it to Emma.

"A detachment of the 37th New York brought in a prisoner who had this on him. McClellan was most interested. Here, read this item," said the Chaplain, pointing to a headline. Emma read, with Kate looking over her shoulder.

Richmond, Virginia
April 29, 1862

Timothy Webster was hanged in Richmond today after being convicted, tried and sentenced in a Confederate court. The hanging was carried out in spite of a warning by President Lincoln that if the execution took place the Union would have no choice but to seek retribution on Confederate spies.

Webster became the first American to be hanged as a spy since Nathan Hale.

At Webster's hanging, the rope broke and he had to be hanged a second time. Just prior to the second hanging, Webster said, "I die a second death."

According to head of Secret Service, Allan Pinkerton, the elimination of Webster leaves a large gap in intelligence gathering for the Union.

"I don't understand. What has this to do with Frankie?" Kate asked her husband.

"McClellan says that Webster's death leaves a hole in military intelligence for the Union. Little Mac needs someone to gather information behind the Rebel lines before the army can attack," explained Chaplain Bee.

"But what of Professor Lowe's reconnaissance balloons. Surely they can scout out the enemy position from the air better than one spy on foot," said Emma.

"Can't see enemy positions from a balloon when the army's in the woods. Little Mac also wants to know the weapons and the enemy's plans for movement. Can't get that kind of information from a balloon observation," said the Chaplain.

"I must ask again, dear. What has all this to do with our Frankie?" Kate asked.

"McClellan has asked me if I know of anyone with sufficient moral courage to undertake a spy expedition behind the Rebel lines. I thought of Frankie immediately," said the chaplain to his wife as though Emma wasn't even there. No one spoke for a moment and then Kate turned to her friend.

"What do you think, Frankie? It is a situation of great danger," said Kate, frowning. "Should you get caught, then . . ." Kate's voice trailed off, leaving the thought unspoken.

But Emma had already considered the idea, with all its fearful possibilities. She thought of James now and his belief in the Federal cause, his conviction that in the end, slavery must be abolished. By becoming a spy, she could help save lives. One person, just one brave soul who could bring to the commander the military secrets of the enemy could be of more value than an entire brigade of soldiers. This was a great opportunity, a mission, a sacred trust. *Emma Edmonds--this is the war adventure you wanted to be a part of--get in there and do your duty,* she thought to herself.

Emma reread the newspaper article and felt charged with purpose. She turned to Chaplain Bee.

"I should like to accept the responsibility, Chaplain. Please recommend me to General McClellan," she said.

That night, Emma dreamed that she was in a great battle. But this time, she ran into it instead of away from it.

To General George McClellan
War Department Headquarters
Washington D. C.

I forward to you the name of Franklin Thompson (Company F, Second Michigan Volunteer Infantry Regiment) as a candidate for the secret service. I am of the opinion that Private Thompson has sufficient moral courage to undertake such duties as are required and the ability to act unselfishly in a crisis. In addition, he is a skilled horseman and marksman, and is capable of filling the position with honor and advantage to the Federal Government.

> *Henry Bee, Chaplain*
> *Seventeenth Michigan*

Chapter 11
Emma Goes to Washington

The carriage in which Emma, Kate and Chaplain Bee were riding moved slowly through the cobblestone streets of Washington. The city teemed with men in blue, officers and politicians, and men and women who had come to the city to work in the hospitals and wartime bureaus. Pennsylvania Avenue was torn up and workers were busy installing tracks for a new street railway. The carriage stopped in front of Number 217, the headquarters of the Secret Service of the United States and the War Department.

Soon the three were ushered into a room where the Generals awaited to cross question "Franklin Thompson." Emma stepped confidently into the room. General McClellan, Commander of the Army of the Potomac, stood near the window. Behind the desk a few paces away from McClellan, stood Generals Samuel Heintzelman and Thomas Meagher.

"Are you prepared to answer our questions freely and without reservation, Private?" asked McClellan after the Chaplain had introduced "Private Thompson."

"Yes sir," said Emma. There was only one thing that Emma had no intention of revealing--that her name was an alias she had adopted to disguise her sex.

"And what leads you to seek a career in the Secret Service, Private?" asked General McClellan.

"My devotion to the Federal cause. I am determined to assist to the utmost of my ability in crushing the rebellion," said Emma.

The Generals exchanged glances, and McClellan nodded, satisfied with her answer.

"Can you shoot from a horse, Private?" asked McClellan.

"Been hunting since I was a boy on the farm up in New Brunswick. Chaplain and Mrs. Bee can attest to my marksmanship," said Emma. It was true that few men of the 2nd Michigan were better shots with a rifle or a pistol than Emma, and she was proud of her skills.

"Reconnoitering's risky business. More chance of getting killed as a spy than in a battle, Private," said General Meagher.

"A soldier of honor doesn't ask what risk there is, he goes where duty calls. I am an honorable soldier, sir," said Emma.

"If you're caught, you'll be hung just like Webster," said General McClellan.

"When Chaplain Bee told me about the job, I knew I was your man, sir. If I'm to die in this war, it makes no difference if it's by noose or minie ball," said Emma.

The generals were satisfied with her answers, and once again Emma was asked to take the oath of allegiance to the United States of America. She did so this time with Chaplain Bee and Kate on either side.

Emma had three days to prepare for her first assignment behind Rebel lines: to gather information about the enemy artillery and their plans for future movement against the Army of the Potomac.

"God be with you Frankie," said Chaplain Bee as they parted.

"If there's a bullet out there with my name on it, it will find me, and there's not a thing I can do about it," said Emma.

"Can't say I hold much with the Presbyterian notion of predestination, Frankie. Better to put your faith in God and ask for divine protection," said Chaplain Bee.

"I'll leave that up to you, Chaplain Bee," said Emma.

The Bees returned to camp, leaving Emma in Washington for espionage training. First, Emma met with McClellan's intelligence advisor, Allan Pinkerton, who taught her some of the tricks of the espionage business.

"Two disguises will serve you for most missions, Private. First is the woman's disguise. With your build, you should pass through the lines as a woman with no trouble at all," said Pinkerton.

Pinkerton was dead right about that, thought Emma.

"A second disguise, and one that has never failed my operatives, is to go as a Negro. Negroes have never betrayed a Yankee spy among them," said Pinkerton.

Emma knew that Negroes were often used to construct the Rebel fortifications and breastworks. What better way to learn about the enemy's fortifications than to actually work on them? But Emma puzzled over the Negro disguise.

"Negroes with some white blood can look just like you, Private, only with dark skin. Darken your skin and get yourself a darkie wig. You'll pass, no problem," assured Pinkerton.

Pinkerton also taught Emma how to use a cipher system for encoding messages to be telegraphed. If the message was intercepted, no matter, for only the recipient had the key to deciphering the scrambled words. Finally, the great spy master showed her how to conceal in her clothing sketches and written messages that must be smuggled out of enemy camp.

Early on the morning of her third day in Washington, her spy training now completed, Emma began her transformation. First, she went to a barber and had her short hair shaved close to her head. On the way back to her hotel, she purchased a suit of plantation clothing just like the garb she had seen the contraband wearing in camp. Next, came the coloring process--head, face, neck, hands and arms she rubbed with nitrate of silver until her skin turned deep brown. Only one more item was needed to complete her transformation. Emma pulled on a straw hat over her shaved head and went out of the hotel into the street of shops to find it.

"Well, boy, what can I get for you?" said the shopkeeper.

"Massa send me to you wid dis yere money for a darkie wig," said Emma.

The shopkeeper looked at her and squinted, then looked at the money she held in her dark hand.

"What does he want of a darkie wig, now, boy?" asked the shopkeeper.

"Don't know for sure. Dat's my orders. Guess it's for some 'noiterin' business," said Emma.

"Reconnoitering business, you say. All right then. You tell your massa I'll get him one. You come back here at two o'clock this afternoon and pick it up."

That evening, Emma, now wearing a new wig of real Negro hair, started back to the army camp near Yorktown to test her disguise. She went immediately to the Bees' tent and found Kate within.

"Will you hire me, ma'am?"

"Don't know but I might," said Kate, looking up from her mending. Emma watched her friend's face for a sign of recognition, but she saw none. "Can you cook?"

"I can cook anythin' I eber seen."

"How much do you think you can earn in a month?" asked Kate. "And what is your name?"

"Name's Ned, and I reckon I can earn ten dollars easy nuff."

"Well, let's try you out for a month and we'll see," said Kate, and as it was supper time, Kate showed "Ned" the flour, pork, beans, a small portable stove, and skillet.

"We like warm biscuit for supper, Ned. You get to work, and I'll go fetch the Chaplain."

Emma grinned. She had passed the first test. Kate had not recognized her.

When Kate returned a half hour later, she found Ned stirring the biscuit dough with a spoon.

"Hold on there, Ned. I thought you said you could cook anything you'd ever seen," Kate said, and took the spoon from Ned. "Biscuit dough's got to be kneaded with the hands, not stirred with a spoon. Here, watch me. Like this."

Kate turned the dough out of the bowl onto the floured board atop the medicine chest and began to work it into a smooth ball.

"Now you try," said Kate, dusting the flour from her hands.

"Sorry. Can't make biscuits with my colored hands. Then I'd have white hands and you'd have black biscuit," said Emma, dropping her Negro dialect.

Kate looked at her closely. "What did you say, Ned?"

Emma pulled off the wig and smiled at Kate. "Don't you know me, Kate? It's me. Frankie."

"I would sooner mistake you for a darkie pretending to be Frankie than vice versa. I'm completely fooled!" exclaimed Kate, and she doubled over in laughter.

"Shh. You must keep my secret," said Emma, pulling the wig back over her head. "I leave tonight for the Rebel camp."

"Surely not until we..." Kate began, but stopped when her husband stepped into the tent.

"Hello dear," she greeted him, planting a kiss on Chaplain Bee's cheek. "This is Ned. I've hired him to cook, but it seems he doesn't know how to make biscuit, so perhaps he can do something for you for his pay," said Kate, and she winked at Emma.

"Well, well," said the Chaplain. "Perhaps you can black my boots tonight. I shall need them early in the morning."

Kate's eyes met Emma's briefly, but then Kate turned quickly away lest her laughter give away "Ned's" secret.

"All right, Massa Chaplain," said Emma. "I allers blacks de boots over night."

Early that evening, Emma blacked the Chaplain's boots and left them at the tent door. At nine o'clock, just as the red sun was dropping over the horizon, Emma put some hard tack in her pocket and started on foot for the enemy camp.

Chapter 12
Behind Rebel Lines

At nine thirty that evening, Ned, alias Franklin Thomas, alias Sarah Emma Edmonds, passed through the outer picket line of the Union Army. By midnight, Emma had reached the Rebel lines, and though she passed within a few yards of a Rebel picket, he had not seen her. Emma took it as a good sign that her mission would go well. When she was within a half mile of the Rebel camp, she lay down on the cold, damp earth to await daybreak.

A hand shook Emma's shoulder, and suddenly she was awake and on her feet. She must have dozed off in the early morning hours. Now her heart pounded in her breast as she shook away the dullness of sleep.

"Who you belong to and why you not at work?" asked an old bearded black man standing over her. A half dozen more blacks stood nearby, eyeing her. Emma smelled hot coffee and bacon and her mouth watered in spite of her fear.

"I dusn't belong to nobody. Ah's free," said Emma.

"Nobody free here, boy. You best come with us," said the old man. "We takin' food to the pickets, and then we come back fo' you" he said, handing her a cup of coffee and a piece of corn bread.

The sun was strong on her face as she munched her cornbread waiting for the party of blacks to return from their errand. Then she marched with them right into the Rebel camp. No one stopped her.

The blacks set to work immediately on building an enormous breastwork fortification. Emma imitated her companions, hauling the heavy gravel in wheelbarrows up to the eight-foot parapet. The day grew hot as the sun climbed higher in the sky. Though the other workers were a talkative bunch, Emma remained quiet for the most part, not trusting her Negro dialect to go undetected.

At noon, the Rebel overseer brought cornbread and whiskey and the Negroes ate their lunch, sitting on piles of dirt and gravel. Though Emma's hands were blistered from wrists to finger ends, she continued to labor for most of the afternoon, and when finally she was not able to take up the wheelbarrow alone, she discovered that her companions were quick to help out.

When darkness came, the overseer released the blacks from their toil. Although she longed to join her companions in sleep, she steeled herself to do what she had come for. After soaking her blistered hands in the cool water of a nearby stream, Emma scouted the Rebel camp. Her first task was to get a sense of the strength of the enemy's weaponry.

From the cover of the woods at the edge of a clearing, Emma began to count the guns. She gazed in sheer amazement at the cannons, lined up wheel to wheel, and beyond them were covered wagons which held supplies and spare ammunition. In the darkness, it was hard to distinguish each individual weapon, but there were Rebel soldiers nearby so she dared not move closer. A rough estimate, then, of the guns.

She counted cannon first. These cannon looked odd, not like cannons of the Union Army, and suddenly Emma realized that these were not cannon at all. Why, they were nothing more than tree trunks painted black, propped up to give the appearance of cannons. These were the guns that had struck fear into the heart of McClellan!

Emma thought about the army and how it had been scared away from fighting these last months. All because of a bunch of dead trees smeared with pitch? By the looks of the rotted ends, they'd been sitting there a while too. The Union soldiers called them "Quaker guns" because the Quakers were known never to shoot any gun.

Emma finished her survey of the fortifications and quickly sketched an outline of the completed breastworks. Then she ciphered the report she would telegraph to McClellan.

Ciphered message:

Regular complete heavily give seven fifteen include and cannons is sketch armed appearance howitzers cannons guns mortars Quaker fort works outer that forty fourteen fort.

Deciphered message:

Fort guns include fifteen cannons, fourteen mortars and seven howitzers. Forty Quaker cannons give appearance that fort is heavily armed. Outer works sketch complete.

Emma put the message and sketch of the outer works into the inner sole of her shoe and then returned to the Negro quarters. Emma slept soundly that night, and the next morning was once again wakened by the grey-bearded black man.

"Yous be askin' for a whippin'. Get up or yous miss the work crew," said the old man, and he kicked the sole of Emma's shoe to get her attention. Emma had not dared to remove her shoes while she slept for fear of losing the sketch and ciphered message if someone took her shoes. Now she sat up stiffly and gratefully accepted the cup of coffee and corn bread the old man handed her.

She winced as the hot metal of the battered tin cup made contact with her blistered hand. She set the cup down on the ground and inspected her palms. They were swollen and tender, and a few open sores oozed. She wiped her palms on her grubby pant legs and winced again. No way she'd be able to resume her duties on the fortifications today. Pinkerton had told her that no black person had ever betrayed a Yankee spy among them. Today, Emma would have to test the truth of that remark.

While she finished her coffee, Emma looked around among the blacks, desperate to find someone to exchange places with. Yesterday, she had noticed a young boy fetching water from the stream to carry to the troops. Now she found the boy preparing for his day's work and she approached him.

"What's you name?" she asked the boy. His smiling face and bright eyes showed his pleasant nature.

"Ah's Cuff," said the boy.

Emma returned the boy's smile, but her voice dropped to a whisper, the Negro dialect all but forgotten. "Cuff, I need your help. Change places with me for today. My hands are sore, and I fear the massa's whip if I don't report to the digging."

Emma held out her oozing palms so the boy could see. He drew back when he saw them, then looked at her face, his smile gone.

"Yous be needin' some salve for dem hands," the boy said.

"Change places with me today. Just for one day. Please, Cuff," Emma pleaded. Then she reached into her pocket and pulled out five dollars in greenbacks, which she offered the boy.

"Please Cuff," she implored.

Cuff drew back, his eyes wide as he started at the money. "I help you. I can't take you money, cuz I neber had so much money in all my life. You take my place for today. Yo hands be betta tomorrow," the boy said, and handed her his pail.

"Oh, thank you Cuff," said Emma, relieved, and she tried to press the money on the boy again but he refused.

"You ain't really what you say you is, is you? You is a girl," Cuff said.

Emma tensed. Slowly, she nodded. "Don't tell anyone," she pleaded.

"Neber," said Cuff, and he left her standing there. She stuffed the money back into her pocket, and picked up the water pail.

If Cuff had seen through her male disguise, did he also see through her African disguise? Could she escape the scrutiny of the soldiers she would supply with water today?

The black dye had not worn off yesterday. Despite the hard work in the heat of the day, Emma perspired very little. If it rained, though, she'd be in trouble. Emma looked up at the slate gray sky.

But the second day in Confederate service proved to be much easier than the first. The morning was cool and cloudy, and the stream was not far. Emma took advantage of her leisure to lounge among the soldiers and she paid close attention to their discussions. She learned the number of reinforcements that had arrived and where they were from, and she committed the information to her memory until she could be alone to write it down.

At noon, the soldiers were much excited by the arrival of General Lee. Emma watched as the grey-bearded stocky man was greeted warmly by his army. To her astonishment, the General rode right up to where she was drawing water and stopped his horse in front of her, as though he sought her out in particular. Emma's heart hammered in her chest.

"What is your name, son?" the General asked, not unkindly.

"My name Ned, sir," said Emma, looking at the horse's hooves, not daring to meet the eyes of the man who questioned her.

"A drink of water for Traveller, if you'd be so kind," said Lee, dismounting and handing the reins to his assistant. "Some oats too, when you have time. It's been a long ride," said Lee before he strode off.

Emma took care of Traveller, and thought him a fine specimen of a horse, strong and sturdy, a proper war horse for a General. She thought Lee didn't look much like a great general, but then Little Mac didn't give one the impression of a warrior, either. Looks alone were no indication of what lay underneath, as Emma knew very well. As she resumed her duties, Emma listened to the speculation around her.

"Lee has come to inspect the fortifications. Battle could be any time, now, I 'xpect," said one soldier.

"I heer'd the Captain say the fort's not good enough. McClellan's guns open on us and we're done for. They got too many guns, is what," said the other.

The Rebels grew agitated as evening fell. Some change was afoot, and Emma mingled with the men, filling canteens, listening to their conversation. At about five o'clock, General J. E. Johnson arrived at the Rebel headquarters for a meeting with Lee, and shortly after, the Rebels began to look gloomy as a report circulated that Yorktown was to be evacuated. Nearly 150,000 Rebels prepared to withdraw immediately. No time to spare, now. Emma had to report the information immediately to General McClellan, but she would have to wait until nightfall to make her escape. Four more hours.

Emma went about her business, fetching water and filling canteens. Her mind was busy formulating a plan to cross the Rebel picket lines, so she paid little attention now to the soldier's conversations. She already had the only piece of information that could matter--the Union Army need not advance on Yorktown, for the Rebels were leaving.

At nine o'clock, Emma prepared to leave. She filled her own canteen, and put a piece of cornbread into her pocket for the journey. It began to drizzle, but no matter, since she wouldn't need her African disguise much longer. But she would be wet and cold for she dared not cross the picket lines with even a blanket, for fear of arousing suspicion.

As Emma made her way to the Negro quarters for the last time, she passed a group of soldiers gathered about a campfire. She tensed at a familiar voice, and as she approached the men, the campfire illuminated the speaker's face. Emma saw that it was the sutler who came regularly to the Federal camp to sell newspapers and stationery.

Two Rebel officers stood on either side of the sutler, studying a piece of paper. Probably selling newspapers to the Rebels, too, thought Emma, and they'd be wise to count their change as she always did. But as she drew closer, she saw that the sutler was showing the Rebel officers a map of the entire works of McClellan's position.

Traitor! Emma hunkered down in the shadows to listen. Emma remembered that often the sutler would sell all the wares he had brought with him and then he'd hang around headquarters for half a day before he returned to Washington. No wonder, he knew so much about the Federal fortifications!

"They lost a splendid officer through me since I left you last," the sutler said boastfully. The men were passing a bottle of whiskey, and their voices grew louder as the whiskey disappeared. One of the Rebel officers slapped the sutler on the back in congratulations and the sutler grinned his corn kernel smile.

"How'd you get him so's our sharpshooter could pick 'im off, Sam?" one of the officers asked.

"I heard him say at headquarters that he was goin' to visit the picket line at two o'clock, so I hurried and told our men that they should capture him. Should've captured him cause he had some valuable information. But they shot him instead," said the sutler.

"No matter, Sam. One less Yankee officer is of no consequence. We got you at Yankee headquarters to get all the valuable information we need," said the officer, and he passed the bottle.

"Still, it was a pity to kill such a man as Lieutenant Vesey, even if he was a damned Yankee," said the sutler, and he threw the empty bottle into the fire, smashing it.

Emma was stunned. It wasn't a random bullet that had killed James! He had been set up by the oily sutler. Emma pulled her hat low and turned her eyes to the ground as the sutler walked past her, so close that she could smell his stench.

"Your life is not worth three cents in Confederate scrip, peddler," she whispered to herself. It had begun to drizzle and Emma knew that her time as Ned was at an end. She had to leave now.

From Emma's *Memoirs:*

> *I thanked God for that information. I would willingly have wrought with those negroes on that parapet for two months and have worn my skin off my hands half a dozen times to have gained that single item. He (the sutler) was a fated man from that moment...*
> *The Female Spy*, p. 117

Chapter 13
Battle of Williamsburg

Two days later the Federal troops were in pursuit of the retreating Rebel Army. McClellan, for once, had wasted no time in acting upon his intelligence report. This time, the information had come from Emma.

The Federals moved forward steadily toward the enemy in a torrential rain. Ordered to reinforce Hooker, Emma's regiment marched for eight miles over the muddy roads. In the ensuing battle, Emma found herself once more under orders to remove the wounded from the battlefield just outside Williamsburg. Emma worked tirelessly and was horrified by what she saw: blood trails on the grass where wounded men had dragged themselves to cover; men with arms and legs shot off, unable to crawl, lying on their backs, waiting to bleed to death; a frantic horse dragging its dead rider by one foot still lodged in the stirrup.

During a lull in the fighting, Emma took cover in a stand of trees, waiting for an ambulance to come from the rear to receive the next cargo of wounded. Bullets whizzed around her. Emma could see bodies among the trees, but she dared not venture out from cover.

A branch snapped close to her head, and a spurt of dirt shot up in front of her, and she dropped to the ground for cover, face pressed against the rich Virginia soil. Cold gathered around her heart and her mouth went dry. She turned her head and breathed heavily, gasping for air.

Then there was a pause in the shooting, as though everyone decided to reload at the same time. Emma lifted her head and looked out over the body strewn field in front of her. Ten yards away, a Colonel from her own regiment was sitting with his back against a tree, motionless but groaning pitifully. The stretcher bearers had reached him, and Emma crawled over to help just as the bullets began to whiz around her once again.

"I'm hit," said Colonel Evans, wincing in pain, but there was no blood to indicate where the Colonel was wounded. Emma helped the stretcher bearers carry the Colonel about a quarter of a mile to where the field hospital was set up. They were exhausted when they finally set the stretcher down and gently raised the wounded man off the stretcher and laid him onto a blanket on the ground.

"Where are you hit?" asked the surgeon, as he began to remove pieces of the Colonel's outer clothing. Emma helped the surgeon remove Colonel Evans' jacket and trousers, but still did not locate the wound. The officer was in such agony, he appeared unable to answer. Emma straightened and watched the surgeon as he examined the Colonel's limbs and torso for wounds.

Suddenly, the doctor stood up and looked grimly at his patient. "Colonel Evans, you are not wounded at all. You had better return to your command," said the surgeon.

The Colonel looked the doctor in the eye and gasped, "Doctor, if I live to get out of this battle, I'll call you to account for those words."

"Sir, if you are not with your regiment in fifteen minutes, I shall report you to the General," said the surgeon before he moved on to the next patient, a boy whose belly had been torn open.

Emma turned and left the spot, disgusted at Colonel Evans' cowardice. No one understood better than Emma that what you saw sometimes turned out to be something else. In the future, she would make sure that a man was really wounded before she risked her own life to help him off the battlefield.

The Battle of Williamsburg was finally over, Fort Magruder was silenced, and the Stars and Stripes floated from the Rebel works. Although the Federals had won, Emma's regiment had suffered heavy losses--one out of every five soldiers had been killed or wounded. Now came the sad business of identifying and burying the dead. Emma wandered among the bodies, looking for wounded to transport to the hospital.

By late afternoon the dead lay in long rows, their ghastly faces covered by handkerchiefs or coats. Soldiers were digging trenches in which to bury the mangled bodies. An exhausted Emma wandered to the edge of a cornfield for one final look around. Near a long dead oak tree, several of the burial detail stood apart, leaning on their shovels, watching a small brown mongrel that was tied to a nearby tree. The dog reminded Emma of her dog Maggie back in Canada, and she approached the cowering animal in hopes of comforting it.

The mutt just looked at Emma and began to howl pitifully.

"What's the trouble?" asked Emma softly, reaching out to touch the animal.

"That hound belonged to Johnny Reb here, and he's a snapping at us for buryin' him," said one of the men.

Emma moved closer and scratched the dog behind the ears, and the dog looked at her mournfully but stopped its whining.

"This dog been fed?" Emma asked the soldiers.

"Don't know," said one of them.

Emma patted the dog on the head. "I'll find you something to eat soon. You let these men get on with their work now," she said. The dog crouched down then and stared at the grave of his master.

As darkness descended, light criss crossed the battlefield as ambulance details continued their search for the wounded. At some point, Emma found Kate sitting with a wounded soldier lying beneath a tree. The soldier's eyes stared into the distance and at first Emma thought the soldier was dead. Then she saw him take a great breath and turn his eyes upon Kate. Relieved to see her friend, Emma called for a stretcher to remove the wounded soldier.

"Leave him be," said Kate, as Emma leaned over the man. She saw that he was wounded in the belly. Severe wounds to the head chest and belly were set aside--there was no time to waste on men who wouldn't survive

Kate gave the man water from her own canteen and Emma and Kate moved on, looking for those who had a chance.

A little farther on Emma found a young man's body in a trench, partially covered with earth. She would not have recognized him in the lamplight but for the ring he wore. She recognized the boy as one of her own regiment, so she removed the ring to send to his mother. She was sorry the burial detail had not covered him with earth, but after this day of death, one more corpse didn't make much difference.

"A pity. A pity, that's all," whispered Kate, as she and Emma moved among the bodies, both Yankee and Confederate. Kate wept openly. Emma wished she could. Near the stream, a young Negro boy lay groaning on the bank. Emma lifted the lamp to better see his wound, and was shocked to recognize her friend Cuff from the Rebel camp, the boy who had traded his water bucket for her shovel. When the boy saw her Federal uniform, he quieted some.

"Shh. Now. I will help you. Where are you wounded?" Emma asked; and she thought she saw a glimmer of recognition in the boy's eyes.

Cuff stopped his groaning and grabbed Emma's arm. She saw that his leg had been shattered, but that the wound would probably not be fatal so she called for the stretcher bearers. When she returned to the hospital, she would ask the surgeon to give this boy special attention. She moved on.

At the hospital, Emma worked beside Kate all through the night. The floor ran with blood as the surgeons amputated arms and legs, throwing the discarded limbs into a pile as if they were no more than chicken bones after a feast. Emma was numb with exhaustion. The great adventure she had set out upon, the struggle she had come to believe in, now seemed a tragic waste of life and limb.

The next day, before Emma fell into an exhausted sleep she fed the Rebel dog she had nicknamed Scout, and then she wrote in her journal.

From Emma's *Memoirs*:

Oh, war, cruel war! Thou dost pierce the soul with untold sorrows, as well as thy bleeding victims with death. How many joyous hopes and bright prospects hast thou blasted; and how many hearts and homes hast thou made desolate! As we think of the great wave of woe and misery surging over the land, we could cry out in very bitterness of soul--Oh God! how long, how long!
The Female Spy, pp. 128--9

Chapter 14
Emma Befriends a Rebel

May 25, 1862
To: General McClellan
The enemy is moving north in sufficient force to drive General Banks before him; precisely in what force we cannot tell. He is also threatening Leesburg and Geary on the Manassas Gap Railroad, from north and south; I think the movement is a general and concerted one--such as would not be if he was acting upon the purpose of a very desperate defense of Richmond. I think the time is near when you must either attack Richmond or give up the job, and come to the defense of Washington. Let me hear from you instantly.

President Abraham Lincoln

May 25, 1862
To: President Lincoln
Telegram received...the time is very near when I shall attack Richmond.

McClellan pondered the President's orders to attack, but it was too soon, too soon. All reports indicated that the mass of Rebel troops were still near Richmond. McClellan needed information about Banks' position and force, and what he might expect for troops at Manassas, and he needed this information before he could attack.

"Summon Private Franklin Thompson immediately," McClellan said to his aide, who rushed out of the tent on his errand.

Once again Emma prepared to become "the eyes of the army." This time she decided to try a new disguise. In camp Emma and Kate bought pies, cakes, and other treats for the wounded from an old Irish woman who followed the Army of the Potomac. Emma had amused Kate with her mimicry of the old woman. Since Emma's own mother was of good Irish stock, Emma had no difficulty with the brogue. Now, she decided to disguise herself as one of the "rale ould stock of bog trotters."

The old Irish peddler agreed to sell Emma one of her dresses, as well as her cakes and pies and the basket she used to carry them. Emma paid her well for the goods. Then Emma packed the sweets, the dress and a head kerchief into the basket and strapped it to her back. She scratched Scout behind the ears and told him to "stay," mounted Rebel and started off in the direction of the enemy as soon as it was dusk.

It didn't take long to find the road that led to the Rebel lines, and she headed south along it. When she reached the Chickahominy River, Rebel waded into it and the water rose, soon covering his feet and knees. The animal lunged and Emma felt the icy water soaking her clothes as Rebel's legs churned away. When they reached the other side, Emma dismounted and gave Rebel a farewell pat and sent him back across the river where he would find his way back to camp.

The night was cool, and Emma shivered in the swamp air as she removed the basket from her back and opened it. Even though the basket had been tied high on her back, the dress inside was as soaking wet as the clothes she wore. Nothing to be done about it. It was now time to don her disguise.

Quickly, a shivering Emma removed her soldier's uniform and pulled the wet, worn gown over her head. The fabric smelled of smoke and sweat, made more pungent by the drenching of the muddy Chickahominy. She wrung the water out of the head kerchief as best she could and tied it around her short hair, knotting it tightly under her chin.

A chill shook Emma as she lay down on the ground to await daylight when she could present herself to the enemy pickets and ask admission as a fugitive fleeing from the approach of the Yankees.

The first thing Emma noticed when she awoke was the stink of her own wet clothes. Her limbs were stiff and sore and she felt hot, so hot. She opened her eyes, trying to remember where she was. Rays of light filtered through the tall trees, and a rabbit scampered under a nearby bush, startling her. Emma sat up and looked around her. Roots the size of tree trunks coiled out of the water of the Chickahominy Swamp. Grayish brown moss hung heavily from the trees. The swamp was filled with shadows and the mists swirled in the sunlight. The air was humid and sat heavy in her chest. Emma stood up and felt dizzy, and immediately sat down again. She wished she had some quinine to treat her fever.

Emma's stomach cramped with hunger. At least she had the cake and pie she had brought to sell. Maybe she would eat a bit and then rest some more until she felt better. But Emma found she was too tired to unpack the basket, and she drifted off into a feverish sleep.

This time, gunfire awakened Emma. The sky was overcast, and Emma had no idea how long she had slept. Was it hours--or days? Cannon fire reverberated through the swamp, shaking the very ground upon which she lay. The armies must be skirmishing on the edge of the swamp, Emma thought. Her fever had somewhat lessened, but Emma was painfully hungry now, and she searched her pockets for hardtack, the square tough crackers issued as rations. Some men made a decent dish with them called skillygalee, by soaking the crackers in water until they were soft, then frying them in pork fat. You'd almost think you were eating meat. Emma's stomach grumbled. No hard tack in her pockets.

She got up stiffly, and opened the basket where she had stored the pies and cakes and was dismayed to see that they were soggy and moldy from their river crossing. *Better to die upon the scaffold at Richmond or be shot by Rebel pickets than to die of starvation in the swamp,* thought Emma, as she rallied her strength. If she was to survive, she must get out of the swamp.

Emma headed slowly in the direction of the cannon fire, using the sounds of the battle for her compass. Once, she was seized by chills so severe that she had to stop and sit, leaning against a tree, her teeth chattering until it seemed the very tree against her back shook. When the chills stopped, the fever came again, but at least Emma could walk through the fever. She felt dirty, starved, exhausted, and every bone in her body ached. She pressed on, and by dusk she was out of the swamp, trudging down a narrow dirt buggy path with her now empty basket, following the sounds of battle.

Emma followed the path to where it forked, one fork leading to a wider, dirt road and the other ending at a small, white house. Emma turned towards the house. A stone chimney was built up one side of the house, but no smoke curled from the stack. Emma was disappointed. She had hoped for a meal at best, or at least a drink of cool water. Emma adjusted her head kerchief and headed for the house.

Everything was quiet as though the property was deserted, but Emma wanted to make sure before she went inside. Cautiously, she circled the building and approached the house from the back. With her dirty sleeve, she rubbed some of the grime off a window and peered inside. Something on the floor moved, causing Emma to jump back from the window. Rats, she guessed, hearing no sounds from within. In a few moments she peered through the window again. This time she could see a man sleeping on the floor underneath a patchwork quilt. One of the man's arms rested on top of the quilt, and that arm was clad in the gray uniform of the Rebel soldier.

"Halloo in there," called Emma, in her best Irish brogue. "Can ye spare a bit o' bread for Bridget?"

She tapped on the glass, and the man on the floor stirred, but didn't make any sound.

Emma went around to the front of the house and opened the door. The man on the floor looked at her, a sheen of perspiration on his brow. She went to where he lay on the straw tick and knelt by his side.

"Is it wounded ye be?" she asked.

The man smiled weakly. "Not wounded, thank God. Sick. Rest of my company retreated when the Yanks attacked at Cold Harbor. I hid here."

The man spoke in a hoarse whisper and he appeared weak and pale, poor man. He probably hadn't been able to prepare meals in his condition, but then Emma hadn't had a bite for more than two days herself.

"The owners be comin' back to feed ye soon, p'haps?" Emma asked.

"No. They left two days ago. They feared the Yanks. They left some food. It's over there," said the soldier, pointing to a cupboard hung on the wall.

Emma looked around the room. At one end was an open fireplace. The family had been kind enough to lay a fire for the sick soldier, at least, before they left, but it had not been lit. Emma lit it now, and then went to the cupboard to get the food. Inside, she found flour and cornmeal and some tea packed in a basket. As exhausted and sick as she was, Emma soon had the fire blazing and began to bake a hoe cake. On the hearth she heated a pan of water for the tea.

Emma sipped the tea as she fed the sick soldier, and he seemed to gather strength from his meal. So did Emma.

"How did you get here? There's fighting all around. You're in danger here, old woman," the Rebel said. He looked to be about thirty, was tall and thin. His hazel eyes seemed large in his pale face as he watched Emma. She recognized the signs of typhoid fever in those eyes, and she wished she had some medicine to soothe him.

"Me name is Bridget and I be sellin' me pies and cakes to the soldiers," said Emma.

"Allan Hall from South Carolina," he said, raising himself up on one elbow. "Whose side you on?"

"Sides! Blarney! I'm on no one's side. Me thinks it scandalous the way Americans be killin' each other this way," said Emma.

"Easy enough to end the war. All the North has to do is leave us alone," said Allan Hall, and he lay back again, pale and trembling. The food had apparently only temporarily revived him. After a few moments, Emma raised the Rebel's head so that he could take another sip of his tea.

"Still, it be too bad to see this great nation split in two," she said after a while.

"All we want to do is govern our own states and mind our own business. Is that so bad?" he said, looking at her.

Emma thought about all the death and suffering she had seen at Manassas and Williamsburg. "Couldn't you have worked something out?" she asked.

But the man didn't answer, for a chill seized him and he lay on the floor, his teeth chattering in spite of the warmth of the house and the hot brick Emma had placed at his feet. Emma tucked the quilt around him and curled up next to the fire and fell asleep herself.

Sometime after midnight, Emma was awakened.

"Bridget. Please come near."

It took her a few seconds to realize where she was and that Allan Hall was awake and calling her. Emma arose and went to him. Allan Hall's face was white in the flicker of the fire that still blazed in the hearth. She couldn't have slept for more than a few hours then.

"And what be the matter with ye, me friend?" asked Emma.

"I fear my life is slipping away, and I do not want to die alone. Sit with me, please Bridget."

Emma knelt beside the man and reached for his hand. His pulse was weak. He was still now, as if in sleep, but when Emma looked at his face, she was startled to see that Hall's eyes were open and he was gazing at her.

"Is there somethin' ye be needin' now soldier?" asked Emma.

"If you ever pass through Confederate camp, ask for Major McKee of Ewell's staff. Give him the ring which you will find in my pocket," said Allan Hall, his voice barely a whisper now. Emma reached into the man's coat pocket and drew out a gold finger ring. It was emblazoned with a crest or seal of some kind, but contained no gem stone. She put it in the pocket of her dress.

When she looked again at Allan Hall's face, she saw that his eyes were still open and he was watching her closely.

The dying soldier then put his hands together, and smiled a mute invitation to prayer. Emma could hardly refuse. She knelt beside him, and in her own voice, for she could not pray in a false voice before God, Emma Edmonds prayed for the salvation of Allan Hall's soul just as she had done for the souls of so many dying men in the Yankee hospitals. A few weeks earlier those men and Allan Hall had been arrayed against each other, yet in death they were all brothers because their faith in God was the same.

When she was finished, Emma rose from her knees. Allan Hall reached for her hand, and said weakly, "Please tell me who you are. I cannot, would not, betray you."

Emma drew back, startled. She could not tell him the truth, but neither would she lie.

"I will tell you later," she said. Allan Hall smiled languidly and closed his eyes as much to say that he understood

Emma dozed again, but could not sleep. Finally, she got up and went to the window and gazed out into the darkness, but there was no moon or stars, only the pitch blackness. All Emma could see was her own reflection in the dirty panes of glass, and she was startled at what she saw--a stranger's face seemed to be looking back at her from the darkness.

At dawn Emma checked on her patient, gave him some water, but knew that he was almost gone. She stood close by and looked down upon the face of Allan Hall. There lay before her the enemy to the Government for which she was risking her own life. He might even be the man who had taken the life of her beloved James. Yet, as she looked upon Hall the enemy, she did not feel hate or anger or resentment. She saw only a sick and suffering man whose health she would gladly restore if she could.

Allan Hall died just as the sun crested over the trees, streaming into the house through the dirty window panes.

Emma closed his eyes and straightened his rigid limbs. Then, folding his hands across his breast, she drew the quilt around him and lay down near the body of the dead man and fell into a deep, dreamless sleep.

Chapter 15
A Close Call

When Emma awoke, it was morning again. She had slept for a full day and night. She spent a few moments beside the body of Allan Hall. Then she cut a lock of hair from his temple and took a packet of letters from his pocket, pulled the quilt over his face and bid him farewell.

After a breakfast of tea and gruel, Emma made a search of the house, looking for anything that would help her improve her disguise. In the pantry cupboard she found mustard and pepper, and in a drawer of a writing stand, she found a pair of green spectacles and a bottle of red ink. She gathered these items together.

With the mustard Emma made a strong plaster about the size of a dollar coin, and tied it on one side of her face with her head kerchief. She could feel the mustard burn its way into the thin flesh of her cheek. Dipping her forefinger into the bottle of red ink, she painted a red line around each of her eyes and put on the green spectacles and an old hooded cape she found hanging on a peg.

In the house, she found a number of other things that an Irish peddler might carry, for once she reached Rebel lines she expected to be searched. Into her basket Emma packed blankets, the rest of the tea and flour, the pepper, and Allan Hall's ring, letters and the lock of hair which she wrapped carefully in a piece of newspaper. Finally, Emma removed the white cotton curtains from the windows and tucked them around the contents of the basket.

On her way out of the house, Emma took a final look at Allan Hall and silently thanked him. A Rebel soldier's ring and letters would be sufficient passport to get her safely into the enemy camp. She left the house carrying her heavy basket and set out along the road.

Emma had walked about five miles before she spotted the enemy picket guard. She sat down beside the road to get ready. First she removed the mustard plaster from her cheek and fingered the painful blister. Then she opened the basket and took out the pepper which she rubbed into her eyes until the tears ran down her face. Finally, she tore a piece from the white window curtain and tied it to a stick. Surely, her disguise would excite the guard's sympathy so that she could pass into the enemy camp.

Emma rose and headed towards the picket guard, waving her flag of truce before her. As she came near, the guard raised his gun but signaled her to come near.

"Where you going, old woman," he drawled. Though his question was abrupt, the man was smiling, and Emma realized that she must present a ludicrous diversion for the bored picket.

"Och! I wish I wez at home wid me family in Ireland. But as it kinnot bee, I am jest runnin' from the Yankees," said Emma, wiping away some of the pepper tears from her face. The blister stung from the salt of her tears. She sneezed twice and blew her nose loudly.

"You all seen Yankees today then?" the guard asked, his smile dropping instantly.

"Nay, not today. But I am fairly kilt wid this onnathral war. We poor crathurs of wimen that's heartbroken intirely," said Emma, and she was rewarded as the guard's face softened once again.

"And where might you all be goin' on this road with the fightin' about to begin?" the soldier asked.

"I need to git to Richmind, where me darlin' girl'll take me in," replied Emma.

"Then, pass, old woman. But best you all keep movin' and not plan to spend the night in our camp. One of our spies just reported that the Yanks have finished building bridges over the Chickahominy. They're about to attack, and Jackson and Lee are ready for them."

Emma couldn't believe her luck at discovering this bit of information, and she took it as a sign that her mission would go well. The guard then went on to tell her how many masked batteries they had.

"There's one that'll give 'em fits if they come this way," said the guard, laughing as he pointed to a brush heap by the roadside. Emma stared at the camouflaged weaponry and made up her mind at once. It was absolutely necessary that she find out as much as possible today and make her way back to Federal camp tonight before the impending battle.

"Och! I thanks ye," said Emma, as she left the guard.

When she arrived in the Rebel camp, Emma stopped at a tent where some soldiers were cooking some meat and asked for a bite.

"Got lots of meat, but ain't got no salt, old woman," said one of the soldiers, giving her a piece of meat and some bread that tasted as though it was made of boiled rice and cornmeal. "Reckon you can eat it without salt," he said. Emma chewed on the meat and listened as the man and his companions talked about their plans for the coming battle, for they talked of little else, ignoring the old Irish woman in their midst. Finally, she heard the piece of information she had been waiting for. The commanding Rebel officer was named Major McKee.

Behind the Rebel lines, these men were her enemies. But Allan Hall had not been her enemy. He had been her companion in suffering for a day and a night, and she fully intended to keep her promise to him.

"Wheer might I find Major McKee?" Emma inquired after she finished her meal.

"He just got back from settin' a trap for the damn Yankees," he replied as he led her to headquarters.

She found Major McKee seated behind a large map-strewn table where his command post had been set up under an awning. He stopped writing and looked up at her when she reached the table. Emma curtseyed and reached inside her basket and removed Allan Hall's ring, the packet of letters, and lock of his hair, and placed them on the Major's table.

"Where did you get these things, old woman?" he asked.

"Master Hall asked me to bring his things to ye, Gineral," said Emma. "He died las' night, but I wuz by his very side as he passed on."

Major McKee lifted the ring and then set it upon the stack of letters and took up the newspaper packet that held the lock of hair. Carefully, he unwrapped the paper and stared at its contents, touching it gently as though it was a lock of hair from his own child. He drew his hand over his rough face and wiped the tears from his eyes.

"You are a faithful woman, and you shall be rewarded for your kindness," he said to her.

The Major turned aside and after unlocking a small wooden box on the edge of his desk, he drew out a ten dollar bill.

"Captain Hall was a valued colleague and good friend. Can you go to the house and show my men where Hall's body is?" asked the major.

"Och! For certain, as I've jist come from there today," said Emma.

"If you succeed in finding the house, I will give you as much more," said the Major. He took Emma's hand and put the money into her palm, closing her fingers around it.

Emma stared at the money in her hand. She could not bring herself to take a reward for doing a final favor for Allan Hall. Emma was surprised to hear him called Captain Hall, for she had not realized Allan Hall was an officer.

Emma put the money on the table and saw Major Mc-Kee's smile flatten, taking on the appearance of a saber cut across his face. His eyes turned steely as he glared at Emma. Too late, she realized her error in refusing the money, and she felt a chill colder than that which came with her fevers.

Emma's heart pounded and she tasted fear. The Major glared at her suspiciously.

Emma needed no pepper now, for terror drove her tears. The Major took a step backward when Emma burst into a fit of weeping, crying "Oh, Gineral, forgive me! But me conshins wud niver give me pace in this world nor in the nixt, if I wud take money for carryin' the dying missage for that swate boy that's dead and gone--God rest his soul. Och, indade, indade I niver cud do sich a mane thing, even if I im a poor woman."

The Major's expression softened and he patted Emma on the back as she continued to weep. After a while, he seemed satisfied with her story.

"Then at least take the money for showing my men where to find Captain Hall's remains," said Major McKee, and he pressed the ten dollar bill into Emma's hand. This time she took it and made a great show of thanking him.

Major McKee asked her to wait while he ordered a detachment of his men to accompany her to the house to retrieve Allan Hall's corpse. When he returned with the men and their horses, he ordered a horse saddled for Emma.

It was late afternoon when they rode out of the Confederate camp. As they rode away, Major McKee shouted, "Now boys, bring back the body of Captain Hall if you have to walk through Yankee blood to the knees." Emma shuddered at his words, even though the sun was hot on her back.

On horseback, they made their way cautiously along the road Emma had traveled by foot earlier in the day. Emma rode at the head of the silent, nervous detachment. The sun began to set behind the western hills and the deepening shadows were fast gathering around them as they came into sight of the little white house. As they drew near, they saw no sign of an approaching enemy.

"Corporal, dismount and proceed to the house on foot. The rest of you, spread out and guard all approaches to the house until we know it's safe," ordered the Sergeant. Then he turned to Emma, and in the same commanding tone told her to ride on down the road a little way.

"If you see or hear anything of Yankees, ride back quickly and let us know," he said.

Emma turned her horse away from the house and set off down the road. When she could no longer see the house, she rode the horse at the top of his speed until he was white with foam. As she plunged her horse into the Chickahominy River, she tossed aside her basket and watched it float off in the muddy current. Emma had something more important to take back to the Federal camp.

Chapter 16
A Visit with Nellie

Sunday, June 1, dawned clear after two days of thunder storms and torrential rains. At seven fifteen, gunfire signalled another day of fighting, and the Battle of Fair Oaks raged fiercely on that day until noon.

"Franklin Thompson" was ordered to help remove the dead and wounded from the field. Arriving at the scene of battle at about ten o'clock, Emma could do little more that look upon the terrible scene. She watched General McClellan ride along the battle front to the men's cheers that told as plainly as words that their commander was beloved even in the midst of this desperate struggle.

When the fighting stopped, the Federals had won, but at a terrible price for more than fifteen thousand lay upon the field. By evening, most of the wounded had been removed to what was called the "hospital tree" near Fair Oaks. Under the high branches of the huge oak lay the wounded, awaiting the medicine or the amputating knife as each case required. The ground around the tree for several acres was drenched with blood, and the men were laid so close together that it was difficult to pass among them.

Emma worked under the hospital tree far into the night. She had not seen her friends Kate and Chaplain Bee all week, and when she finally had asked their whereabouts, she was told they had gone home on furlough. They had taken the dog, Scout, with them. Well, when the work was done on this day, Emma would also ask for a furlough. God knows, she needed a rest.

She wished she could go home to visit Magaguadavic, but she still feared her father and didn't want to make trouble for her mother. Besides, she had not heard from her mother for many months and Mother had asked Emma not to write again until Emma could sign her own name to the letter. Instead, Emma decided to request leave to visit the various Federal military hospitals of the Peninsular to secure supplies and learn what she could about caring for the sick and wounded.

On June 5, "Franklin Thompson" received a leave of absence. On a beautiful, sunshiny day, Emma saddled Rebel and headed out of camp alone. Her first visit would be in Williamsburg, which had two hospitals, one for the Confederates and one for the Union. Emma was delighted to find Nellie, her wounded hand still bandaged, but otherwise well and content and working at the Federal Hospital. Here, Nellie had charge of patient intake, and she grouped her patients together depending on their illness and temperament.

"This is the pleasure department," said Nellie as she and Emma walked side by side through the hospital. Most of the men were sitting up in chairs, reading or talking amongst themselves. Some were sitting at a table playing cards and laughing.

"These men we visit with books and flowers. They will recover and go home to loved ones soon."

Next, they passed into a darkened room that Nellie called the pathetic department. "These men we visit with beef tea and wine and general consolation," said Nellie. Emma didn't need to ask why. The patients were lying in beds lined up on both sides of the room. A few men were sitting up in bed, talking with visitors, probably loved ones who had traveled long distances to see them.

"And this is the working department. Most of the newer patients are brought here first," said Nellie as they went into the third chamber. In this room, patients awaited the surgeon's knife. Nellie and Emma went from bed to bed, trying to soothe the patients as best they could, dispensing bandages and plaster and opiates when they were needed.

Nellie seemed to have a special way of soothing even the worst cases. Emma thought it odd that Nellie should give such comfort to men who had so recently been her enemies. She watched Nellie as she comforted a boy about to have his leg amputated.

"It hurts. Don't want to die. Mother."

"Shh. There now. You won't die."

"Feelin' weak. Leg hurts. Big hole there."

"I'll stay with you, and I'll be here when you wake up."

"Don't want 'em to cut off my leg."

"Shh. Drink this. You'll feel better soon."

"Don't want to die. Hurts."

"Nobody dies. The doctor's here to make it stop hurting. Here's a nice smelling cloth, now."

"Smells funny."

"Shh. I love you. Breathe. And remember, I love you."

The boy breathed in the chloroform and after ten minutes he only had one leg. Nellie stayed with him the whole time, though the boy could not know that.

"Nellie, did you ever consider if it might have been that boy who fired the shots that killed your own menfolks?" Emma asked later.

"Doesn't make any difference, Frankie. Consider men who go to war. What do they do?" asked Nellie. Emma looked at the men in the hospital beds, the men Nellie so lovingly cared for.

"They fight each other," said Emma.

"Yes, but they fight according to a code of honor. And when this war is done, they will all be called heroes, Rebels and Yankees alike, because they observed the code and fought with honor. It won't matter then which side they fought on, but rather that they fought the battle with honor," said Nellie.

It seemed to Emma that she had made an important discovery about war. No one was really against each other in the fray, for they were all bound together--every soldier, Rebel and Yankee, every surgeon and nurse, every spy, even the dog on the battlefield who guarded his master's grave. The same code of honor that bound them all was the sense of duty that called on them to do what they believed was right.

"These men," said Nellie as she waved her arm in an arc that took in the room, "they're all alike, really." It was a hint that she didn't include Emma with them--meaning, all men.

Emma looked Nellie straight in the eye. Neither woman spoke for a time.

"I'm glad you came, Frankie," said Nellie finally.

"Me, too, Nellie," said Emma.

Bullets weren't the only shots Nellie had fired at Emma. But unlike Nellie's bullets, her words hit their mark.

From Emma's *Memoirs:*

There are luminous planets which are viewed by the aid of their own light, others there are which are seen through borrowed light. So it is with individuals. There seem to be some who have scarcely any light of their own, and who shine by the reflection of the light of others; while others there are who possess an intrinsic and inexhaustible source of sunshine, which renders them not only self-illuminating, but capable of irradiating those around them.

The Female Spy, p. 85

Chapter 17
An Orchard Grave

Emma spent two days and a night with Nellie, learning all she could about the hospital. After leaving Williamsburg, Emma headed down the Peninsular for Yorktown.

Although the day was once again bright and lovely, Emma grew despondent as she approached the site of the old camp where she had spent her last days with James. Emma looked around her at the site. The old hospital building was gone. Nothing was left but a heap of ruins.

"James, my friend," she whispered, as she rode over the places she had last shared with James. Tears rolled freely down her cheeks as she toured the deserted camp, and the memories came flooding back. She urged Reb on until they reached the spot where her friend was buried. Emma tied Rebel to a fence rail and headed into the peach orchard which had become the camp cemetery.

She wandered through the orchard looking for the one pear tree that grew there amidst the peaches, for that is where they had buried James. When she found the spot, she sat upon the mound of earth and, head in hands, let the tears come freely. She now felt none of the hate that she had felt when she last visited the spot, only an emptiness and sorrow that shook her inner core.

Emma turned her face skyward and stared into the limbs of the pear tree that shaded the grave. That pear tree was as out of place in a peach orchard as a Canadian was in this war between the States, she thought. *This wasn't your war, James. Why did you have to die in it?*

As she sat upon James' grave in the brilliant sunshine, she remembered James' words. "This war isn't about where

you're from. It's about how you feel and what you think
about things."

"Good bye, my James. I loved you well," Emma whispered, and turned her back on the grave.

Dying was not predictable. Emma had always known
that. She had seen little, puny men, no bigger than herself,
suffer and recover from terrible wounds. Then there were
others, big, strong and healthy lads who died pitifully from
measles or fever or even from a little scratch that suddenly
became infected. One died when it was time, that was all.

From Emma's *Memoirs*:

*But there was a spot, undisturbed, away in the corner
of the peach orchard, under an isolated pear tree, a
heaped up mound, underneath which rested the noble
form of Lieutenant V. It was sweet to me to visit this
spot once more. I knew that in all probability it would
be the last time; at least for a long period, perhaps
forever.*
                         The Female Spy, pp. 199-200

From Yorktown, Emma went to White House Landing,
a tidy village with neat, well kept houses and shops. The
town was laid out with broad, tree-lined streets which were
swept clean as a floor. The military camps on the outskirts
of the village were set up in long rows of snow-white tents
that gleamed in the summer sunshine.

Emma spent two days visiting the Federal hospital in
White House Landing and prepared to return to camp as her
furlough week was almost used up by then. The weather had
stayed fair, and Emma anticipated a pleasant ride back to

camp, but as she saddled up Rebel for the return, she saw that he was limping.

"Not enough cigar butts in your diet this week, eh Rebel?" she said to the horse as she examined his hooves and found some swelling in his front forefoot. "We've got to get you back to camp to toughen you up," she said straightening up. Rebel nuzzled her shoulder. There was nothing to be done but take the train, for Rebel couldn't be ridden.

Emma requested transportation for herself and Rebel on the provision train destined for Fair Oaks Station. After making sure that Rebel was loaded and comfortable, she went to an empty passenger car and settled down for the trip. A train ride would not be as pleasant as riding through the countryside on Rebel, but she looked forward to the trip nonetheless.

The train steamed out of the station at two o'clock and Emma, lulled by the rhythmic rattle of the rails and the swaying of the passenger car, dozed where she sat. She woke just as the train slowed to pass though Tunstall's Station.

Emma sat up and looked out the window at the landscape. From the distance, she heard the shrill whistle of another train approaching the station from the opposite direction. The train in which Emma was riding slowed to a crawl and switched off the track to wait for the approaching train to pass.

Suddenly, a sharp volley of musketry sounded, as though from the approaching train which came thundering on like a streak of lightening. The speeding train passed on the tracks just a few feet from Emma's window. In the coaches of the other train, Emma saw signs of wild confusion. She heard the sounds of groaning men above the screeching of the engine, and she saw the uniforms of the Federal army.

Suddenly, the train in which Emma was riding began to move. After switching rails, it was now headed in the direction of White House Station right behind the renegade train they'd just passed. A half hour later when the train pulled into the station, Emma jumped out of the car and ran across the platform to the other train where Federal officers were disembarking in confusion.

"Jeb Stuart's cavalry it was. They must've circled our boys to attack us at Tunstall!" said one of the men in blue. "Caught us from a bank that overlooks the railroad cut just below the station."

Wounded soldiers were being helped down from the passenger cars. Emma saw by the uniforms that many of the passengers were officers of high rank who would have been a rich prize if the train had been captured.

Emma hoisted herself up into one of the passenger cars. Inside were many wounded who lay moaning in the aisles and on the seats. She began to organize relief, directing the able bodied in carrying the wounded off the train so they could be treated.

Within an hour a military surgical team was at the station, and Emma fell into her role as nurse, helping to dress wounds and dispense water and opiates. As she began to bathe the sooty face of one man, she paused in shock. The man, slightly wounded in the shoulder, was dressed in civilian clothes. The face was that of the sutler she had seen in the Rebel camp at Yorktown, the Rebel spy who had bragged about bringing about James' death.

"I ain't no soljah. Jest tryin' to sell my papers and got caught in the fray," he said. Emma couldn't speak.

She continued to wipe the grime from the man's face until she was sure it was the sutler and finally he grinned, showing his yellowed teeth as he recognized her from the Federal camp.

"Well, well. If it isn't the boy soljah. I see you still ain't shavin' boy," said the sutler, wincing in pain.

She helped the doctor to remove the man's coat and shirt, and he groaned in agony but his eyes never left her face.

"Don't be takin' away my coat now, soljah boy. I can clean it up good as new. No sense buyin' me a new shirt, neither, cuz I can be patchin' the hole," said the sutler.

Emma looked at him in disgust, hating him, but she set her teeth and turned her attention to the wound. The bullet had passed clean through the shoulder, and the wound was soon cleaned and dressed. He'd survive the bullet, more's the pity, thought Emma. She'd make sure he didn't survive the noose.

As soon as the wounded were taken care of, Emma visited the provost marshal and made known the fact that there was among the wounded a Rebel spy who required immediate attention. When the provost marshal and a guard went to the hospital and searched the sutler's pockets, they found satisfactory proof that "Franklin Thompson's" statement was correct. Inside the heel of the sutler's boot were drawings of McClellan's battle plans.

Chapter 18
A New Disguise

The summer of 1862 was filled with days of awful fighting around the Rebel capital of Richmond. Emma was busy nursing the wounded. Although the last bloody engagement was counted a Federal success, McClellan thought it best to retreat across the Peninsular and through the dreadful Chickahominy Swamp where Emma had suffered from malaria.

A week after the Army of the Potomac arrived at their new camp in Harrison's Landing, Emma received a message to report to headquarters of the 2nd Michigan. It was from Colonel Evans the coward she had helped to carry off the field at the battle of Williamsburg. Emma found Colonel Evans alone as she entered the tent. He rose when she stood before him.

"I am informed that you are one of the persons who carried me off the field when I was wounded at Williamsburg. You must have witnessed the infamous conduct of Dr. Bonine and heard his insulting remarks," said the Colonel, pacing back and forth in front of her.

Emma did not reply. Colonel Evans disgusted her and she smiled in contempt. The Colonel stopped his pacing and looked her full in the face.

"See here, boy. Why do you not answer me?" said the Colonel, seizing her roughly by the arm.

"Pardon me, sir. I was not aware you asked me a direct question. I understood you to say that you were informed I was one of the persons who carried you off the battle-field at Williamsburg. That is correct," said Emma.

Colonel Evans released her arm and resumed his pacing. "Then you saw the treatment which I received and heard the abusive language which Doctor Bonine used on that occasion," he said.

"I saw Doctor Bonine examine you thoroughly and I heard him say, 'Colonel, you are not wounded at all. You had better let these boys carry you back to your regiment. If you do not return within fifteen minutes, I will report you to the General," said Emma, staring straight ahead, waiting for the Colonel's explosion of anger. It didn't come.

Colonel Evans reached in his pocket and pulled out a paper and handed it to Emma. "Perhaps you can be persuaded to change your memory, boy. If you will put your name on this document, I will personally reward you handsomely," said the colonel.

Curious, Emma took the paper and read the carefully printed document:

> *This is to certify that Colonel Evans has been infamously treated and maliciously slandered by Doctor Bonine while said colonel was suffering from a wound received at Williamsburg battle. Two of the undersigned carried him bleeding from the field, and witnessed the cruel treatment and insulting language of Doctor Bonine.*

Emma almost snorted in amusement as she read the paper. Then, handing it back to him, she said "Colonel, I must decline signing this paper." Touching her hat in a mock salute, Emma turned and left the tent. I'd sooner be court martialed myself than add to the glory of Colonel Evans, she thought. Emma remembered that two Vermont soldiers had been caught skulking during the same battle and sentenced to have half their heads and faces shaven and the buttons cut off their shirts. Then they were drummed out of camp to the jeers of their comrades. Colonel Evans, in her opinion, deserved the same treatment, or worse, because he was an officer.

A month passed and everything remained quiet at Harrison's Landing. Then on August 14 orders came for evacuation. The Army of the Potomac was on the march, this time to the assistance of General Pope who was facing annihilation in the Shenandoah Valley. Pope's troops were fighting with few provisions except for the fruit, green corn and vegetables they found in the fields. They couldn't hold out much longer. Once the Army of the Potomac made camp, "Franklin Thompson" was summoned to headquarters.

"We need to know the number and locations of Confederate troops as quickly as possible," said General Heintzelman.

"Yes sir. I need a day to get a disguise," said Emma, excited by the prospect and filled with purpose.

"Another week and Pope's army may be lost. Come back as quickly as you can. I'll do whatever I can to speed you on your way," said the general.

"I shall need train passage to Washington," said Emma, already formulating a plan.

Five minutes later, Emma left General Heintzelman's tent, with a full purse and orders to take the train from Warrenton Junction to Washington, where she could purchase her disguise. Emma returned the same night and before dawn began the application of the nitrate that would darken her skin. This time she decided to pass through the lines as a female contraband.

All week, Emma had observed small groups of free blacks passing along the road that led to the Rebel lines. The Union pickets let them pass in safety as they did most other civilians. Emma thought to pass into enemy territory with one of these groups.

Emma left her tent before daylight and began walking slowly along the road towards the rebel lines. By ten o'clock she caught up with a group of nine contraband, all women and children.

As they walked along the dusty road, Emma learned that these black folk had been recently freed after their master was killed in the fighting at Williamsburg and the mistress could no longer manage the plantation.

"How you take care yo'self, now yo have no massa to look afta yo?" asked Emma of one old woman.

"Gosh a-mighty, girlie. Been takin' car of myself and massa for twenty years. Guess I can take car of me all alone now," she replied.

"Then why you goin' to the Rebel camp now?" asked Emma.

"I goes to be wif my daughta and granchillun. I rather live in bondage wif them then be free wifout 'em," said the old woman. "What you goin' for anyway?" she then asked.

"Ah's always been free," said Emma.

The group had no trouble passing the Rebel pickets, and when they entered camp a Rebel officer asked if she could cook.

"Ah cooks, but ah not a good baker," said Emma, hoping to avoid the biscuit making activity that might expose her white skin. She was assigned to kitchen duty with three others.

"We need enough rations cooked to last us till we whip them Yankees and reach Washington," said the soldier as he escorted the group to the camp kitchen.

All morning long, officers visited the kitchen and stopped outside to talk among themselves about the coming battle. Emma listened closely.

As the officers ate, they talked. And because they were excited with the battle preparations, they sometimes forgot to be careful about what they said. By afternoon, Emma had the very information she had been sent for.

Emma memorized what she heard, including the battle plan for the next day and the number of troops expected to arrive during the night. Although she now had what she came for, she dared not return to the Federal camp that night without causing suspicion. Better to wait until the next morning when she could walk out of camp as easily as she had walked in that day.

Early the next morning, Emma rose and helped prepare breakfast for the headquarters staff. She offered to carry a tray of steaming coffee and bacon to the commanding general. It would be her last duty before she could sneak out, she thought. Headquarters was a tent fly stretched out among the trees that formed an awning. Underneath were a folding desk and several camp stools. Emma set the tray on the desk and removed a coat from a nearby campstool, and as she reached to hang it from the awning post, a sheaf of folded papers fell from the pocket of the garment. Emma looked around quickly to see if anyone was watching, but the camp was strangely quiet in the early morning hour as the men caught their last few minutes of slumber before the battle to come.

Quickly, Emma stuffed the papers into the pocket of her dress and pulled her shawl closely around her. Better not wait for the General to return and find his papers missing, she thought. She must leave now before she was caught. Emma headed for the picket line nearest the Union side.

Emma walked slowly, as though she were in no particular hurry. Curiously, no one stopped her, though she passed the spot where the pickets had allowed her entry the day before. She walked straight out of the Rebel camp without a second glance from anyone, and she took it as another sign that the mission was successful.

By the time she was about a mile from the camp, Emma heard shots in the distance, and then alarmingly, the shots came closer. A minie ball whistled into the tree over her head. Someone was shooting at her! She looked around wildly. The minie ball had come from in front of her. Was she being shot at by her own army, she wondered in panic. And then more shots answered, this time from behind her. Emma began to run as she realized she was caught between the two armies.

Running at full speed now, Emma tripped and fell face first into a ravine as the bullets whizzed above her, and then incredibly all was silent. She raised her head and looked around. Up on a rise to her left, she saw the ruins of an old farmhouse. She had better make a run for it if she was to find any real shelter from the bullets. Emma pulled herself out of the ravine and, lifting her skirts, ran as fast as she could to the house. No one shot at her this time.

The old building turned out to be a shell of a house long deserted. Emma reached it just as the firing began again. On one side of the house was an entrance to what was once the cellar, and Emma descended into the musty gloom as a shell burst nearby. The fighting was so close now she could hear the frantic yells of the skirmishers, and above the battle sounds she made out the distinctive Rebel yell which sounded as if it came from an animal rather than a man. Emma collapsed in the damp and moldy cellar as the building above her began to tremble with the reverberations. It was cold and her hands were shaking. Pieces of the stone wall came rattling down upon her and she was afraid the whole building would collapse, trapping her in the cellar forever. A small animal ran over her feet and she jumped, hitting her head on something hanging from a beam overhead. She gritted her teeth to keep from crying out.

The firing, coming from all directions now, grew louder and louder. It was as if both sides were aiming for the house and their single enemy was herself, not each other. Emma shivered in the cold damp cellar and waited for the roof to come crashing down on her.

Soon the firing lessened and then stopped altogether. And after all had been silent for an hour, Emma still sat in the damp cellar, too scared to move. When she finally crawled out, the sun was high overhead, and its warmth flowed into her, giving her strength. "Thank you God," she breathed. There was no time to waste. The enemy aimed to capture Washington today, and Emma had the information to spoil their plans. She hurried back to the road and towards the Federal lines.

Back at the Federal camp, Emma went immediately to General Heintzelman to report what she had learned the day before. Almost as an afterthought, she pulled the wad of papers from the skirt of the dirty, torn dress and handed them to the general.

"Oh, yes. Sir, I was able to take these from the headquarters of the commander just this morning. I don't know what information they contain, or if they will be of any use," said Emma as she turned to leave the tent. She was desperately tired, and beginning to feel shaky with hunger.

"Private Thompson! You have brought me the order for the corps commanders with instructions on how they plan to capture our capital. Well done, Private Thompson," said Heinzelman.

Lee's army was now pressing to capture Washington. There would be no rest for Private Thompson. In ten days, she made three visits behind the Rebel lines, each time returning with valuable information. But these efforts were not enough to push the enemy back. By early September the Union forces had withdrawn to Washington to reorganize. Meanwhile, General Robert E. Lee of the Confederate Army, crossed the Potomac to invade Maryland.

Chapter 19
Battle of Antietam

On September 16 it rained steadily, but the atmosphere in camp was one of excitement. The soldiers had been given several days' ration of food and told to cook it immediately in case there wasn't time in the coming battle ahead. Most, it seemed, were already eating their total supply of food, Emma noticed.

Soldiers who normally neglected their weapons were cleaning and recleaning their muskets and sharpening their bayonets. Some were slicing crosses into the ends of the minie balls so that they would cause more serious wounds, a practice that sickened Emma. She thought about how this war had changed everything for the worse, and she wondered if any of the other soldiers would agree that war degraded just about everything it touched.

Emma thought back to the day when she and her regiment had started on their march to Washington. On that day, there had been cheering and excitement and high expectations for a fast but glorious victory. None of them had any notion of the bloodiness and pain of killing or of the wasteful destruction of the landscape and property that they would leave behind in the wake of battle. True, some of the soldiers seemed to revel in the competition of war, as though it were some great sporting event, but Emma knew that these men were stupid, so she held her tongue. She was by now adept at duplicity, and she counted on it to preserve her until the conflict was over.

September 17, 1862. It would be known as the bloodiest day of the Civil War. The North called it the battle of Antietam. The South called it the battle of Sharpsburg. Emma called it hell.

Emma had discovered that men facing battle feared three things, usually one more than the other two--fear of death, fear of mutilation and fear of cowardice. In pre-battle hours, they grew silent, contemplating their fears and gathering courage. At dawn Chaplain Bee prayed with the men of the 2nd Michigan and reminded them to aim low.

Across camp, Colonel Edward Cross addressed his regiment, pacing back and forth in front of them: "Men, you are about to engage in battle. You have never disgraced your State; I hope you won't this time. If any man runs I want the file closers to shoot him; if they don't, I shall myself. That's all I have to say."

At 7 a.m. they heard the first Rebel yell. By 8 a.m. a white fog of gun smoke had blanketed the entire area, obscuring the enemy position. The acrid smoke burned Emma's nostrils and eyes as she helped to move the wounded off the field of battle, and the horrible noise of the shells passing overhead deafened her.

When it was over, more than 23,000 were missing, dead or wounded, mingling their blood with the rich Maryland soil.

On September 18 they went out on both sides to gather the dead. Although there was no formal truce, nobody fired. In passing among the wounded, Emma stopped by the side of a soldier who had been shot in the neck. She stooped over the young soldier and saw that the wound had already bled a great deal, and although the boy's eyes were open, he was weak from loss of blood.

"I've brought you water," said Emma as she helped the boy to drink. After he drank, he gazed into Emma's face, and his eyes were so intense, Emma could not look away.

"There is something you must do for me when I die," said the boy, "for I know that I am dying."

Emma leaned closer because his voice was faint. "I will do what I can to help you," she said. "Is there something I can send to your family. I will write to them and tell them you fought with honor today."

"I have no family. My only brother was killed today. I closed his eyes but an hour ago, and soon I will be with him. I came to war to fight beside him and now I wish to join him in death, for I am his sister," said the dying soldier.

Emma was stunned. This dying girl at her feet had endured many of the same trials as Emma. Only this girl would soon die, and Emma was as yet unscathed by battle.

"Please bury me with your own hands and help me keep my secret," the girl implored, and then she closed her eyes but Emma saw that she still breathed, though faintly.

"You can trust me to keep your secret," said Emma, but when she checked for the girl's pulse, Emma saw that she was gone.   Later, Emma sat near the grave of the girl she had buried with her own hands.

From Emma's *Memoirs*:

> *I remained with her until she died, which was about an hour. Then making a grave for her under the shadow of a mulberry tree near the battle-field, apart from all others, with the assistance of two of the boys who were detailed to bury the dead, I carried her remains to that lonely spot and gave her a soldier's burial, without coffin or shroud, only a blanket for a winding-sheet. There she sleeps in that beautiful forest*

where the soft southern breezes sigh mournfully
through the foliage, and the little birds sing sweetly
above her grave.

The Female Spy, pp. 272-3

Emma closed her journal and thought about the others
who had died at Antietam. Unlike the girl whose grave
Emma had dug, most would be buried with ceremony and
honor, memorialized in monument and hearts for all time.
Emma guessed death wasn't so bad if you were somebody's
son instead of nobody's daughter.

When President Lincoln visited the battlefield on October
3, he found it still covered with wounded, though most of
the dead had been removed and hastily buried in temporary
graves. Looking upon the scene, he found the justification he
needed to show the rest of the country and the world that the
Union dead had fought for a cause just as important as the
defense of the government. They had died so that an idea
embodied in the word "freedom" could be passed on to all
generations.

Emancipation Proclamation
September 22, 1862

> *That on the first day of January, in the year of*
> *our Lord one thousand eight hundred and sixty-*
> *three, all persons held as slaves within any*
> *State, or designated part of a State, the people*
> *whereof shall then be in rebellion against the*
> *United States, shall be then, thenceforward, and*
> *forever free; and the Executive Government of*
> *the United States, including the military and*
> *naval authority thereof, will recognize and*

> *maintain the freedom of such persons, and will do no act or acts to repress such persons, or any of them, in any efforts they may make for their actual freedom.*
> Abraham Lincoln

Chapter 20
Emma Leaves the Army

The chill struck Emma as she was filling her canteen from the water barrel. She reeled blindly against Rebel, grasped his reins and walked back to her tent, shivering in the warm October sunshine. She lay down on her bedroll and thought *one of these days I won't be able to get back up.* Then suddenly she felt hot. Beginning to sweat, she removed her jacket. She was burning up and her head throbbed. She saw black spots form before her eyes. Would this dreaded ague never leave her alone? Weak and dizzy, she made her way to the hospital where she could treat herself with the quinine that seemed to help relieve some of the symptoms.

She thought of the battles she'd survived with never a wound, and the risks she had taken behind enemy lines and was never caught. Now she lay weak and sick and alone on her bedroll, fearing to ask for help because her sex might be discovered. The old Scottish preacher's words echoed in her head: "A wean that's born to be hung'll ne'er be droon'd." Well, fate be damned. Emma prayed hard that she would not die of the fever.

As her adopted country was divided against itself, so was Emma. On the one hand she believed that what she was doing was right, and that she was indeed duty bound to continue her part in the struggle. On the other hand, she knew that she would have to leave the army if she had any hope of regaining her health. If she left the army, she could free herself from one kind of bondage at least--that of duplicity and ruse and always pretending she was what she was not. If she was to survive, she must emancipate herself from such constraints. Emma made out an application for furlough and sent it to headquarters for approval.

Kate brought her the reply. "Your furlough request was denied, Frankie. Colonel Evans believes you should undergo a complete physical examination and be treated in the hospital here."

She might have known that Colonel Evans, the coward whose paper Emma had refused to sign, would get the upper hand eventually. Oh, how he hated her.

"No. I will not go to the hospital," said Emma.

"You must, Frankie. I shall care for you there myself," Kate said, pleading.

"No. I cannot," said Emma.

"Why not Frankie? Your health won't hold out much longer. You could die. Come to the hospital for rest and treatment," said Kate.

"No," said Emma, and she turned her back on her friend.

Soaked in sweat, Emma lay on her cot and looked out the tent flap at the evening sky. Scout snored softly on the floor beside her. When she finally slept, her dreams were filled with the faces of the soldiers she had tended, and then those faces transformed into the faces of her family. The faces of those who had died--and those who were dead to her. Then the faces disappeared and there was a voice, James' voice, but she couldn't understand his words. She tried to ask what he wanted, but she was too tired and fell back asleep.

The next morning, still weak, Emma pondered what to do. Go to the hospital for treatment and risk exposure? Tell Kate the truth and ask her help in keeping her identity a secret? Confess the truth of her gender to General McClellan and ask for a chance to continue her service after she got well?

She thought of all the sick men she had cared for in the hospitals, and how often they had in their pain and delirium called for their mothers. Emma wished for her own mother now. She remembered long ago looking into the mirror in the parlor and seeing her mother's features in her own-- Emma's own--reflection, and she had been appalled to think that she might have a life as dreary as her mother's seemed to be.

Now Emma tried to picture her mother's face in her memory and found that she could not. Weakly she arose from the cot and went to her haversack and fished around for the small mirror she carried. She pulled it out and gazed into the smoky glass in the dim light. She did not see her mother in the reflection now--she saw a young woman with dark eyes set into a tired, pale face. Dark hair fell over her smooth brow. Though no one had ever called her pretty, Emma thought that if she let her hair grow out to frame her face, she might be considered a handsome woman. *Look at your young lady now, Mother,* she thought sadly. She put the mirror back into the haversack, and pulled out her writing paper and pencil, and wrote a letter to her mother. When she was finished writing, she signed it Emma Edmonds.

On the morning of April 19 before dawn, Emma rose from her cot and began to fill her haversack. She packed her journal and writing materials, her toothbrush and the letter she had written to her mother the night before. Then she removed her Union uniform and put on the dress she had worn when she posed as an Irish peddler. Emma fed Scout and into her skirt pocket she put some hardtack and a piece of dried meat, which would have to suffice for her own breakfast. She would take nothing with her that was not rightfully Emma Edmonds'. After saying goodbye to Rebel, Emma and Scout made their way to the road and headed north.

Epilogue

Franklin Thompson, weary and sick, left the Army in the spring of 1863, for fear hospitalization would reveal "his" true sex. "Franklin" traveled to Oberlin, Ohio, and during convalescence as Emma Edmonds, wrote the memoirs first titled **Nurse and Spy, Or, Unsexed, The Female Soldier**. It became a best seller.

What sense of duty drove Emma to enlist in the army as a male and then assume the dangerous responsibilities of a Union spy?

In her memoirs, Emma offers this explanation:

I am naturally fond of adventure, a little ambitious and a good deal romantic, and this together with my devotion to the Federal cause and determination to assist to the utmost of my ability in crushing the rebellion, made me forget the unpleasant items, and not only endure, but really enjoy, the privations connected with my perilous positions. Perhaps a spirit of adventure was important--but patriotism was the grand secret of my success.

In 1864, near the end of the Civil War, Emma felt compelled to return to hospital duty as the increase in casualties brought forth a demand for competent nurses. Compassionate humanitarian that she was, Emma donated all of her royalty payments from **Nurse and Spy** to the sick and wounded soldiers of the Army of the Potomac.

While visiting a hospital in Harpers Ferry, Emma met Linus H. Seely, a widower from New Brunswick, Canada, then in the United States working as a carpenter. The two fell in love and married on April 27, 1867, in an elegant wedding at the Weddell House in Cleveland, Ohio. The pair had three children, none of whom survived childhood. However, the Seelyes (Emma herself added the third "e" to the name) adopted two boys and raised them lovingly to adulthood.

Emma continued to help other people after her marriage. In 1875, the Seelyes managed an orphanage in Louisiana established for black youths under the auspices of the Freeman's Air Society. According to one source, Emma gave away much of what she earned for the benefit of the sick and poor, and her husband said that Emma "was never happier than when she was doing some good for another."

Eventually, because of continued poor health and financial difficulties, and because she was haunted by Franklin Thompson being branded as a deserter, Emma decided to apply for the soldier's pension rightfully due her for her service as Franklin Thompson.

The case was debated by the House of Representatives in 1884 and House Bill 5335 includes the following statement:

> *Truth is ofttimes stranger than fiction, and now comes the sequel, Sarah E. Edmonds, now Sarah E. Seelye, alias Franklin Thompson, is now asking Congress to grant her relief by way of a pension on account of failing health, which she avers had its incurrence and is the sequence of the days and nights she spent in the swamps of the Chickahominy in the days she spent soldiering.*
>
> *That Franklin Thompson and Mrs. Sarah E. E. Seelye are one and the same person is established by abundance of proof and beyond a doubt.*

Eventually Emma won her battle with Washington, and on July 5, 1884, Congress cleared "Franklin Thompson" from desertion charges, allowed Emma's claims, and adopted a bill:

Granting a Pension to Mrs. Sarah E. E. Seelye, alias Franklin Thompson Be it enacted by the Senate and House of Representatives of the United States of America in Congress assembled; that the Secretary of the Interior is hereby authorized and directed to place on the pension roll the name of Sarah E. E. Seelye, alias Franklin Thompson, who was a late private in Company F, Second Regiment of Michigan Infantry Volunteers at the rate of $12 per month.

Emma died on September 5, 1898, after a final bout with the malaria she contracted and suffered with so much during the war. A loyal dog was by her bed as she suffered, and the neighbors heard the dog howling when Emma finally gave up her life. She is buried in the Washington Cemetery in Houston, her grave marked with a limestone tablet bearing the inscription "Emma E. Seelye, Army Nurse."

How much of this book is true?

Historical fiction is a tricky genre for the writer as well as the reader. On the one hand, the writer wants to tell an interesting story that is historically accurate. On the other hand, the reader wants to know how much of the story really happened and how much is a product of the writer's imagination.

Where Duty Calls is a fictionalized account of a portion of the wartime memoirs of S. Emma Edmonds (born Edmonson) alias Private Franklin Thompson. The major characters and events are depicted pretty much as Emma describes them in her memoirs. Indeed, some of the journal entries in this book are actual excerpts of the memoirs, and the reader will find page numbers cited at the ends of these quotations. Journal entries and letters that are not cited are the product of the writer's imagination.

In the memoirs, Emma does not always give last names. For example, Kate and Chaplain Bee are Kate and Chaplain B. in the memoirs. The cowardly Colonel Evans is simply called the cowardly colonel. James Vesey is referred to as Lieutenant James V. Emma was apparently trying to protect the identities of these people.

A few incidental anecdotes were added by the writer to move the plot along or develop a character. For example, Emma never received James Vesey's watch or any other token after his death, according to her recollections. And although Emma was an animal lover throughout her life, there is no indication that she adopted a dog after the battle of Williamsburg.

Because memoirs are written after the events occurred, both the writer and the reader of historical fiction that is based on such accounts are left to wonder how accurate was the memoir writer's memory. How much did Emma embellish her own exploits in order to put them into a better light, and how much did she change in order to hide events she may not have wanted people to know about? Sylvia Dannett, Emma's biographer, noted that when Emma was asked if her war memoirs could be regarded as authentic, Emma replied, "Not strictly so." However, she claimed that "most of the experiences recorded there were either my own or came under my observation" (Dannett 249).

Further Reading

Selected Fiction about the Civil War
(* denotes reading level suitable for young readers)

Across Five Aprils by Irene Hunt (Berkeley Books, 1965).*

Bull Run by Paul Fleischmann (Scholastic, 1993).*

By Antietam Creek by Don Robertson (Prentice Hall, 1960).

Dog Jack by Florence W. Biros (Sonrise Publications, 1981).*

Fighting Men by John Zubritsky (Branden Publishing Co., 1994).

Ghost Cadet by Elaine Marie Alphin (Henry Holt and Co., 1991).*

Hew Against the Grain by Betty Sue Cummings (Atheneum, 1977).*

In My Father's House by Ann Rinaldi (Scholastic Inc., 1993).*

The Red Badge of Courage by Stephen Crane (D. Appleton and Co., 1895).*

Ride Proud, Rebel! by Andre Norton (World Publishing Co., 1961).*

Rifles for Watie by Harold Keith (Cromwell, 1957).*

The Sacred Moon Tree by Laura Jan Shore (Bradbury Press, 1986).*

The Slopes of War by Noah Perez (Houghton Mifflin, 1984).*

Which Way Freedom? by Joyce Hansen (Walker, 1986).*

With Every Drop of Blood by James Lincoln Collier and Christopher Collier (Delacorte Press, 1994).*

Nonfiction sources concerning Female Soldiers and Spies during the Civil War

Belle Boyd in Camp and Prison by Belle Boyd (Otley and Co., 1865).

Blue and Gray, Roses of Intrigue by Rebecca D. Larson (Thomas Publications, 1993).

Civil War Nurse, The Diary and Letters of Hannah Ropes edited by John R. Brumgardt (University of Tennessee Press, 1980).

Clad in Uniform: Women Soldiers of the Civil War by Wendy King (C. W. Historicals, 1992).

The Female Spy of the Union Army by Sarah Emma Edmonds (Boston, DeWolfe, Fiske & Co.,1864).

The Life of Billy Yank by Bell Irvin Wiley (Doubleday and Co., Inc., 1943)

She Rode With the Generals by Sylvia Dannett (Thomas Nelson and Sons, 1960).

Spies and Spymasters of the Civil War by Donald E. Markle (Hippocrene Books, 1994).

Spies! Women in the Civil War by Penny Colman (Betterway Books, 1992).

An Uncommon Soldier: the Civil War Letters of Sarah Rosetta Wakeman (alias Pvt. Lyons Wakeman), edited by Lauren Cook Burgess (Minerva Center, 1994).

Index